THE OSPREY ANGLERS   Editor: Clive Gammon

SALMON

Michael Shepley

Colour plates by Keith Linsell

OSPREY PUBLISHING LIMITED

First published in 1975 by
Osprey Publishing Ltd., 12–14 Long Acre
London WC2E 9LP

Member Company of the George Philip Group

Series Design: Norman Ball and Paul Bowden

Filmset and printed Offset Litho in Great Britain
by Cox & Wyman Ltd., London, Fakenham
and Reading

ISBN 0 85045 212 0

ACKNOWLEDGEMENTS

Some of the material in this book is based on earlier
published articles which appeared in *Creel, Angling*
magazine, *Angler's Mail* and *Rod and Line*. Photographs
on the Tweed at Kelso are the work of Michael Prichard.
Figures relating to the Thurso were supplied by retired
Head River Superintendent, David Sinclair; and those
relating to the Nith were supplied by James Fyfe,
Secretary of the Nithsdale Angling Improvement
Association.

The flies illustrated on page 37 are of commercial
manufacture and some might be thought
overdressed for normal conditions.

I. EARLY BEGINNINGS

My first contact with salmon was by way of trout fishing as a youngster — fishing one of the upper tributaries of the River Tweed, the Lyne Water. In those days the trout fishing on the stream was free to anyone and ideal for a young lad to learn the rudiments of the sport.

I was fortunate in having a wise old uncle who was a dedicated fly fisher, and my first ever trout rod, a 9-foot split-cane fly rod, was my pride and joy. I spent many trips tempting trout with the fly before succeeding, but I had risen and hooked my first salmon, a tiny parr barely 5 inches long. This stream was full of these fish and I soon learned to shake them off the hook with care, without even touching the fish or removing it from the water.

In May a new fish caught my attention as a trout angler, both on these upper tributaries and in the main river where I had graduated in search of even bigger trout; these were brightly coloured, silvery fish and if you took one, you would take a dozen. They were smolts. I remember in schoolboy excitement killing one such fish somewhat bigger than the average thinking it to be a truly fine wee sea trout until a very understanding angler explained to me the foolishness of my act.

Certainly since those days the upper river has at times seemed almost empty of both parr and smolts but yet the salmon survives. No doubt, with the easing during the 74/75 winter of disease, we can hope for improved spawning for a while at least. The smolts that do make the estuary and the open sea are immediately vulnerable both to predatory fish in the salt water and to estuary seals. Those that make the long journey to the Greenland feeding grounds and back again the following year will run the rivers in June and July as proud slim bars of silver-summer grilse. A fish back from the sea as a mature adult for the first time can either be a grilse, having spent one winter feeding in the sea, or the salmon can extend its stay in salt water and return the following year as a maiden fish.

Grilse generally average around 5 or 6 lb. but there are exceptions at both extremes and occasionally one hears of grilse weighing close to double figures — and others so tiny that they can be confused with sea trout.

I took one such fish on the River Oykel during low water summer conditions on the upper pools above Oykel Falls. The grilse took a single, No. 8 Jock Scott as it floated down the current, inches from the surface. The timing of the wee fish was incredible. The salmon had already shown in a delightful head-and-tail rise which indicates to the angler a possible taking fish. I covered the lie quietly, keeping the fly well upstream of the salmon's station. I was fishing virtually downstream, hanging the fly from the rod tip into the fast current. When the fly was barely 2 feet away from the salmon, a small kype and gaping jaw came almost vertically out of the water and seemed to hang there, suspended weightlessly, until the fly arrived, to be sucked down in a tantalizingly slow movement. It was the most fantastic rise I have ever seen a fish perform.

How I managed to delay the lifting of the rod tip and bent into the fish I don't know. Being virtually below me on the rise, in spite of the loose coil of slack which I had allowed the fish to take, the fly was firmly embedded right in front of the lower jaw — not the safest of hook-holds by any means.

The grilse proved to be the smallest salmon taken from the Oykel that year and just tipped the scales at 2 lb. 12 oz. So as to be in no doubt, scales from the shoulder of the fish were sent down to Dr. J. W. Jones of Liverpool University for confirmation. Anyone seeing the fish would have had little doubt as to its authenticity but there would have been many sceptics thereafter as the tale was told, had this particular angler not had the scientific backing of someone whose book on the life of the salmon is greatly respected in angling circles.* (Further study did reveal, however, that this tiny fish was far from being the smallest ever recorded in Britain and there are two cases of net-caught fish in the Dee, summer grilse that weighed less than 2 lb.)

Perhaps the most exciting time of the salmon life cycle, is in early autumn. Then the fish begin congregating in the lower regions of the rivers, ready for their spawning run to the middle and upper reaches and tributaries beyond, to play out the spawning act which ensures the continuation of the species. Unlike the Pacific salmon, which die after spawning, not all Atlantic fish die, although the act and the deterioration which follows account for large numbers of spawned fish which never have the chance to make the sea again and thus have the opportunity of becoming second spawners.

By September, and even earlier in some rivers, a lot of salmon which have been in fresh water since the spring are well advanced in spawn and the cock fish have already started to take on their tartan 'spawning garb'. I always think that the autumn salmon look superb, especially the cock fish; and how wonderfully close is the match between the salmon's colouring and the autumn colours of the trees on the river bank.

The salmon are often paired up before the salmon rod fishing season closes and it is not uncommon to cover a moving fish only to discover that the successful take has been from the partner fish. One of the nicest stories to relate in that vein came from association water on the River Tweed in November. The angler, an experienced fly fisherman, had seen a fish head-and-tail in the holding lie on the stream, and a carefully placed fly met with an immediate response from the fish. The salmon that had shown originally had not taken the fly but the partner fish had. During the fight, the angler suddenly realized that from time to time there was more than one fish at the end of the line and it was soon obvious that although only one salmon was hooked, its mate was keeping it company as it battled for its life. The fish was in superb condition, well over 20 lb., but was eventually skilfully tailed by the angler to the

* The Salmon by J. W. Jones, D.Sc., Ph.D. (Collins, 1959).

One of the smallest mature salmon ever recorded on rod and line in Britain, a grilse of 2 lb. 12 oz., taken on a low water 'Jock Scott' on the Upper Oykel by the author during his 'student' days as a ghillie on the old Balnagowan Estate.

The authenticity of the catch was confirmed by Dr. Frost of the Freshwater Biological Centre on Windermere, and Dr. J. W. Jones of Liverpool University.

delight of gathered rods who had stopped their own fishing to see the fun and games. Without a word being spoken, the fly was taken carefully from the fish's mouth and as gently as possible the broad flanked salmon was slipped quietly back into the water. With a flip of its tail it rejoined its mate and the pair swam back into the depths of the pool.

That is a true story and a surprising one because — sad to relate — a very large number of the 'anglers' who fish the association water on the Tweed do little else than deliberately rake the pools in an attempt to foul-hook the salmon. This practice goes on in other rivers in Scotland, including some of the summer waters where large runs of grilse come into the rivers in July and August. The visitor to our salmon fishing must be warned until this practice is eventually stopped.

There are other waters, such as the Tay, where anglers given the privilege of stretches like the beautiful fly fishing available to local anglers just above the town of Perth, acknowledge the true tradition of the sport and not only respect the quality of the fishing but the salmon as well. Even when a fish is foul-hooked quite by chance, there is no question of the salmon being retained by the angler. It is carefully returned to the water. This is fly fishing water and most of the anglers there are indeed experts. It is sad to relate that other rods on the town water do take advantage of the heavy autumn runs and the congregating fish shoals within the town itself. Excessive raking and foul-hooking of salmon has not only put at risk the availability of the fishing for everyone but has in most cases chased the genuine angler away.

There are times when salmon will take a fly in what would appear suicide bids to be caught. One notable guest on a highland fishing water, for whom I was ghillying during my student days, had the greatest of difficulty in throwing a presentable line, and no attempt at trying to advise her of the proper control and physical balance of the tackle could improve the performance. I am sure that a competent angler that day might have failed to take a fish; but not our lady friend. With mustered power the fly was hurled out into the stream to land amid coils of knotted cast and floating fly line. The salmon, 'a daft yin', rose 3 feet from the gravelly pool bottom in a beautiful head-and-tail rise, which plucked the fly deftly from the tangled mass, straightened out the cast, and hooked itself as the surprised angler fell backwards on the bank! I pleaded that the fish should be given line but to no avail. 'It doesn't look a big one,' was the reply, and 'this rod is surely strong enough.' My friend proceeded to march the fish backwards out of the pool and up the shingle bank until it was kicking 10 feet from the river not a full minute after taking the fly. I don't know who was more surprised — the salmon, or her poor ghillie!

2. THAT FIRST DAY

There is always an element of magic about the first day of a new salmon fishing season and over the years I have experienced some memorable occasions, not always connected with landing fresh-run fish.

I travelled north from Edinburgh early one mid-January morning, heading for a middle beat on the Tay near Caputh, excited by the prospect of the new season's sport and taking the rods out of moth balls after the winter. There was a crisp frost and early morning mist still on the water as we arrived. With little water, and low temperatures, we hardly expected much action from fresh fish — at any rate until later in the day.

The south bank is densely wooded on our beat and shields the river from the first of the morning sun. The main pool itself is tucked at the foot of a steep brae and as we started to climb carefully down the slippery bank, it was obvious that there were a lot of salmon kelts in the water, as several were jumping all over the pool.

Many anglers will tell you that they don't like kelts. I'm not one of these. For me they've always given good sport on days when spring fish were few and far between, and whether or not a fish has to be returned to the water after the fight is of little consequence. The fact remains that every time a kelt rises to your fly or takes a bait — for me at any rate — there's the same old thrill and excitement as when a salmon takes my lure.

Since ulcerative dermal necrosis (UDN) first decimated our salmon stocks, perhaps the most significant early season fish missing from Scottish waters, has been the kelt. No longer do we have days of aching arms and feel the slight frustration over every fish coming to the bait being a spawned salmon instead of the fresh-run bars of silver of magnificent spring fish. But there is a sign that things are improving. The 1975 season began in Scottish waters in the middle of January on a number of rivers including the River Ness and the Tay. Both waters were running heavy after considerable rain storms and sport was

A true Tay winter fish, taken in mid-January by the author, fishing just upstream of Kenmore Bridge at the mouth of Loch Tay. The salmon, a near twenty-pounder, showed in front of one of the bridge supports, having just run through the stream.
An accurate bait put immediately over its nose produced the hoped for response. It is unlikely that the fish would have rested in that particular lie for more than a few minutes.

Its slight colouration suggests that the salmon came into freshwater several weeks before capture (November/December of the previous year), but was not going to spawn until the following autumn being immature in spawn, unlike the baggot.

This particular fish had outward signs of infection from UDN on its head.

our day of kelts was going to be the last 'day of plenty' for many years. The three rods took over fifty salmon for our short winter day and of these only one, my twenty-first fish of the day, was a fresh-run springer; it was a beautiful, hard, brilliantly silver fish of 17¾ lb.

At this time of year, most anglers prefer to use spinning baits or harling from boats, with large plugs or lures. Certainly salmon are to be found in the quieter water and they tend to lie deep. A slow bait, fished deeply, will do well in these conditions. It might come as a surprise, though, to many anglers to realize just how successful fly fishing can be, even in January. On a number of occasions, we've taken the first fish of the year on the fly from relatively streamy water. The pattern does vary though.

In our fishing on the Tay, there is always friendly rivalry to see who can take the first fish of the day, albeit a kelt, and on opening day in particular extravagant promises of drams and pints to the first bent rod are generally the order of the day. In the rush to the waterside, my bet was a kelt on the first cast. I missed it! I hooked my first fish of the season on the second cast — a 10 lb. kelt. Within seconds, Bill Currie, my host on that day, was into his first fish and Lawrence Keith, the third rod, could be seen well up into the stream at the head of the pool playing another heavy fish. Within minutes my bait was taken again, this time by a different fish altogether. It bored deeply and powerfully and moved well upstream into the current as soon as it was hooked. I doubted if this was a kelt and as things turned out, it wasn't, but it was no springer either.

On the Tay, in particular, it is common to find several classes of fish in January: the true springer, fresh in from the sea, that will be making its way upstream to spawn the following autumn; the kelts which have spawned during the late autumn and winter months and which are now dropping back to the sea in the hope of recovery to return another year; and winter fish which can come into the river as early as the previous October and, indeed, are sometimes caught before the end of the season. Unlike the late autumn runners which are going to spawn, these fish do not mature until the following winter and therefore spend anything up to a year or more in fresh water. These are the fish that give sport to opening rods as far upstream as the top end of Loch Tay at Killin, and in the middle of

affected as a result. It was significant, however, that on one Tay beat at Islamouth, there were eight kelts landed during the opening few hours — probably more than most rods have had for the opening month for many a year. Apart from anything else it's a good indication that the fish are again surviving the rigours of spawning and with luck more fish will be making back to the sea and giving us the chance of larger salmon when they return to the river to spawn a second time.

As we put up our tackle on that first day on the Tay many years ago, we little realized that

January anglers can take clean fish which have been in the river two or three months.

There is yet another class of fish quite common in many of the Scottish waters and in particular, in my experience, on the Tay and on the Tweed, and this is the baggot. These are generally heavy fish averaging anything from 18 lb. upwards that have failed to spawn during the normal season and are, in fact, spawn bound. They are generally powerful fish and put up a good struggle before coming to the bank. They're full-bodied, deep, beautifully shaped fish and firm of flank but their ripeness, dark colouring on the back and steely grey flanks give the angler no doubt as to their identity. Whether returning the fish is an advantage is difficult to say and I don't really know if these fish survive their physical difficulties or not. Some may be late spawners and cut redds successfully later in the year. I've certainly seen salmon paired together on the Tweed in April.

In the salmon pool itself, there is a pattern which allows the angler to anticipate the sort of fish he is likely to take. The spring fish and indeed the unspawned winter salmon are generally found towards the head of the pool and can often be lying in fairly strong currents. The kelts understandably prefer the quieter back eddies and the smoother water at the end of the main run, and down into the tail of the pool, often lying just above the fast water of the next stream. But again, there are significantly two styles of kelt. We found frequently that a fly, fished in the streamier water, produced small, brightly coloured kelts of 5 or 6 lb., invariably cock fish which took a delight in charging the fly and gave a wonderful feeling to the angler on the take. This to me was perhaps the most enjoyable aspect about my own modest fishings on the Tay. I had eleven fish on the fly in one short spell in January — all kelts. It was marvellous fun, covering rising fish and seeing them turn in fast water to engulf a 2-inch Yellow Dog tube with the speed and determination of a springer. Farther down the pool the kelts tended to be darker in colour and bigger and most of the hen fish fell into this category. So you see, salmon fishing to me especially in the opening weeks is not just a simple question of doing battle with one type of sporting fish. The variety of the catch and the ways in which the fish can be lured to the bank cannot be bettered.

3. A WAY OF SPINNING IN THE SPRING

In March, April and even into May, the salmon in our rivers tend to lie in the deeper, slower parts of the pools, rather than in the faster streams. Certainly once the temperature goes up, and the fish move into swifter and better oxygenated water, the technique of fishing for them changes. It is under the first, colder conditions that I now discuss tactics.

The River Tay in Perthshire, and the Cumberland Eden are two of the earliest rivers in Britain, their season starting in the middle of January. An old friend, George Phillips, who ghillied for many years on the Eden in the spring, always used a deeply fished devon, 2½ to 3 inches long, either a Yellow-belly or Blue and Silver, if the water is cold, and changing to something gold (Black and Gold devon), if the sun produced a rise of temperature during the day. The Eden fish are large and an average springer will weigh as much as 19 lb.; they are slow movers to the bait, and the general tactic of fishing deep and slow, with a large spoon or devon is a sound one — the method of making the bait fish as desired varies, however, with the type of water fished.

Both on the Eden and the Tay, boats are used on some beats a great deal, and the bait or baits can be trolled some distance behind the boat, as the boatman works slowly over the known lies. Much depends on the knowledge of the boatman, and the angler has little to do other than play his fish. Bank fishing on the Eden in the spring is done mainly by spinning the lure slowly through the water across and downstream of the angler. On the Tay, however, even the seemingly slow, smooth glides have such a force of water through them, that it is possible normally to cast the lure — which often these days is that excellent Swedish spoon, the 'Toby' — across and slightly downstream, and then 'troll' the bait from the bank, and without winding in at all, let the current work the lure round and over the lies in a natural manner. It is difficult to impart into the lure, by this method, any accelerated movement without affecting the depth at which the lure should be working, and other means have to be found for doing this.

The effectiveness of this additional movement was brought home to me on the Tay at the start of this season, when, after taking a few kelts by the bank trolling method, I decided to cast the

spoon well upstream and about fifty yards out — letting the lure sink, and then spinning it slowly back down, using both the current and accelerated movements induced by the rod. I immediately hit a fish. This method allowed me to vary the speed without changing very much the depth at which the spoon was fishing, and at the same time the lure was still working over the lies at a slower speed than with the bank trolled bait. It was even possible just before the lure came opposite the angler to hang it over a particular lie, and more or less estimate the time of the strike which almost always came at that point.

Once hooked, the playing of the fish varies little from any other time of the year, except that the river is probably running full with melted snow from the hills, and the angler very often finds himself many yards downstream from the point where the fish was hooked, before it is finally landed. The method of landing the salmon is up to oneself, but I never like to use a gaff, especially at this time of the year, because of the number of kelts and the smaller number of unspawned back-end salmon, which are hooked in the early months of the season. Hand-tailing a fish, or using a mechanical tailer, or simply beaching a fish where possible, allow one to return a spawned fish, undamaged and with the shortest delay — and don't forget; put the kelt back head upstream, and hold him in the current until he's strong enough to swim away.

How not to play a salmon! An angler plays a lively salmon on a small west-coast river. The salmon is being held too tightly, the rod is too low, and not 'cushioning' the strain on the tackle from the jumping fish. Correct though — the angler waiting quietly in position, with the net already under the water, once the fish tires. The inevitable happened, however, and the fish broke free.

4. SUMMER - GRILSE TIME!

My first love of Caithness was its game fishing. Several years ago I was introduced to the Thurso River by the secretary of the Dounreay Angling Club, Police Security Officer Duncan Speirs. I wasn't due in my office that particular morning until 9 a.m. Every year at that time it seemed, give or take a few minutes, the summer run of grilse entered the mouth of the Thurso River and filled all the pools and fast stream of the lower beats with its silver harvest. Duncan knew this and the previous week had booked a rod for the first period, 6–10 a.m. on the Monday morning. A strict rota of two rods was at that time allowed to fish, the day being broken into four, 4-hour periods, allowing eight rods to fish in all.

The bay had been alive with salmon for weeks — waiting for the signal of rain. On the Sunday evening, with the river still at summer level, the salmon began nosing their way up the thin water to the first rods. As the tide rose, so too did the number of fish. I don't know whether it was a change in barometric pressure which induced the fish to run, for the rain didn't come until the Tuesday — but they came in their hundreds!

At ten to six on Monday morning, Duncan and I were walking over the fields, avoiding the one with the bull in it, and being chased by some rather fierce cows instead. By six, the rod was up. I was Duncan's guest and he offered me first chance down one of the nicest stretches of fly water I've seen for summer fishing. I declined, being happier to watch him fish the water he knew so well, and asked him to point out the less obvious lies as he fished. We were joined by Jack Robertson, the local tackle dealer, who was to fish the second rod. Jack moved off below the swing bridge to try a slower glide.

Duncan took about half-a-dozen strides, and the loop of the line held loosely in his left hand disappeared as a grilse stopped the fly in the fast water right under the far bank. The rod was raised, the fish was hooked firmly in the scissors. After a spectacular aerial fight the fish was tailed out — 9 lb. exactly the scales showed, an above average fish for the summer run.

It was now my turn. Although the single-hooked Jock Scott had taken the last fish easily enough, I decided to drop down to a $\frac{3}{4}$ inch Yellow Dog tube, an old favourite tattered and chewed by a respectable number of Oykel grilse, and I moved right up into the fast, shallow stream at the head of the pool. On the second cast, the line tightened and kept going. It was nine minutes before I landed that grilse, and it was only about 5 lb. At one stage in the fight it had beached itself on the opposite bank, and that was the first time I've wished a salmon would get back into the river! Duncan lost his second fish and by 8.50 I had taken a twin to my first. All three fish were as shining as new fresh French francs — not more than an hour or two out of salt water, the sea-lice were witness to that. What a way to start a week at the office — in at 9.15 a.m. on tip-toe past the boss's door (it was always slightly ajar), with a couple of grilse tucked into my briefcase!

Since that eventful first trip, I have fished often with Duncan, not only the Thurso River, but many of the multitude of lochans in Caithness, from the tiniest, a mere pond called Loch Glutt, to one of the largest, Loch Watten, with its trout similar to silvery Loch Leven's. It took Duncan several years of tramping the Caithness countryside, fishing and investigating several hundred lochs, rivers and burns, to produce his guide, *Angling in Caithness*, and well worth the effort it is too. Not only does it list the waters the visiting angler can fish, and the methods best suited to the water in question, but in it he captures a lot of the atmosphere of the fishing environment, the rolling moors, the wind, and sometimes the sun.

5. ANOTHER LOOK AT THE THURSO RIVER

The Thurso River rises in the Knockfin Heights on the Caithness/Sutherland county march. Here the ground is barren, flat and expansive moorland, inhabited by the red deer and grouse. From Knockfin, the river gathers strength as it twists and meanders its way to the sea some forty miles distant, draining as it does so some 162 square miles. After less than half that distance, the river empties into Loch More which sixty-three years ago was dammed to provide over 500 acres of stored water. This has had the effect that spates caused by heavy rain in the upper reaches can be prolonged over several extra days, and thus maintain a good fishing height for several weeks without appreciable rain. This has often allowed anglers sport with fresh running salmon when otherwise the river would have been virtually bone dry. It is from the dam downstream that most of the Thurso River's fishings are carried out. If prolonged drought conditions persist, and the river becomes very low, the Loch itself comes into use, when it has returned to its original banks, and again in the autumn the loch fishes well with a rise of water. The whole river can be successfully covered from the bank, and little wading is required.

The river is split into fourteen beats, and these are fished by two rods each per day. The Thurso Angling Association has the whole of beat one, and this can fish extremely well, especially during the start of the grilse run when over ten fish can be the order of the day. The Association may be joined by visiting anglers for a nominal sum, and these visitors may fish in rotation with other local members. Beats two to thirteen are fished in strict rotation by guests staying at the Ulbster Arms Hotel in Halkirk or the Lochdhu Hotel near Altnabreac. As the fishing is extremely popular and is often booked from one year to the next during the peak periods, it is advisable to book well in advance. Apart from June, and early in the season, it is not easy to obtain the odd day's fishing on the off chance that a rod may be available. Beat fourteen which is above Loch More is let separately. The only other part of the river not available to anglers is the series of pools between beats ten and eleven called Lord Thurso's beat which is reserved by Thurso Fisheries, and does not form part of the rotation. Loch Beg forms part of beat thirteen and may be fished from the boat which is provided on the loch.

The rotation system

The rotation system allows two rods fishing together on a particular beat to move downstream by two beats each day, so fishing even numbered beats one week and odd numbered beats in the second week (or vice versa). In this way, a fair sample of both upper and lower water is fished in the one week, and the whole of the fishing water available is covered in the fortnight. The interesting part of this 'jump' rota system is that in certain heights of water, specific parts of the river will fish better than others. It would be frustrating for an angler, say, fishing the bottom beat two, to find that all the fish were being taken on beat thirteen which he might not fish for long enough if he was moving by a beat a day. With the existing rota system, he is soon fishing the upper river, and the fish should still be in a taking mood, while the chap who had the terrific sport on the upper beats is now taking his chance on productive water. The opposite, of course, can be the case, depending on time of year and water conditions, and the whole river contains first-class pools and salmon lies in every beat.

In the early spring, and by that I mean mid-January to the end of February and March, fishing is not so productive, and consequently, there are generally rods available. There's plenty of sport, however, with kelts and it wouldn't be the first time that a lucky angler has gone home with a brace of springers under his belt.

Rules

Fly only is the strict rule on the river, and any fishing with bait, prawn, worms, spinner or spoon is expressly forbidden. The only other real rule on the river is that only two rods fish each beat at any one time; this doesn't, however, preclude two friends or, say, husband and wife, from sharing a rod providing they exercise their right in turn. 'It is understood that anglers will exercise their right to fish in a fair and sportsmanlike manner, and with the high amenities of the area at heart, leave the lunch huts and river bank in a tidy condition free of litter or damage.' With so much livestock in surrounding fields, it is also very important to ensure that all gates are closed after you; the River Superintendent will make sure

A beautiful stretch of fly water on the Logierait Hotel beat of the Tay.

Strong winds; bleak but compelling moorland; open meandering pools where wind direction is sometimes more important than the current; a summer river, bursting with silvery grilse: you are in Caithness.

you don't get directed through any fields with bulls in them!

David Sutherland, the River Superintendent, is in daily attendance at the Ulbster Arms and in charge of all day to day arrangements on the river. He's available to give advice on all subjects connected with the river, and the numbers and weights of fish caught are given to him each day for the record books. Ghillies are available on the river, and for the visitor who hasn't fished the river before, they are more than useful. A month's warning is generally needed, however, before an impending visit if a ghillie is required so that a suitable man can be made available.

All salmon taken, as isn't the case in all fisheries, remain the property of the angler concerned, but Thurso Fisheries always reserve the right to take a cast of any fish weighing 35 lb. or more, and to take scales from any of the fish for scientific or record purposes. It is significant, with the care and attention to detail evident in the management of the Thurso River, that little or no sign of ulcerative dermal necrosis is evident in the stock. Thurso Fisheries have their own hatchery, and also control the nets at the river mouth, thus ensuring an adequate balance.

6. AUTUMN SALMON

With the autumn comes rain — and with the rain, salmon.

The arrival of the heavy fish which make up the back-end run is the time for those who cannot afford an expensive beat on an exclusive river to put up the fly rod, and away to the river bank. There are many good stretches of association water on such late rivers as the Tweed which, in autumn, hold splendid numbers of these big fish.

Cock Salmon (*Salmo Salar*) in breeding colours

Salmon Kelt (spawned-fish) (*Salmo Salar*)

Forty-four pounds of summer salmon from the Kinnaird Beat, taken in 1972, one of the best fish from Scotland in recent years.

fly and heavy line. But, given a reasonable height of water, greased-line fishing, with either low-water dressings or small tube flies, can still do well. Fishing so, I have taken fish as late as mid-November.

But in a big water, sunk fly must be used and most anglers prefer to use flies containing a lot of red or yellow in the dressing. Torrish, Garry Dog, Ackroyd — they all do very well. But there is a danger here — on days of high wind and sweeping rain hundreds of dead leaves are swept downstream, and, as well as being a continual nuisance in fouling the line, they compete with the reds and yellows of the flies. In these conditions I much prefer to fish a dark-coloured fly; the big Stoat's Tail tube fly is a good one.

Search the slower, deeper parts of the pools, and the tails of the long flats. Be ready for the fish that comes up behind your fly as it hangs below you, prior to the back-cast.

A final word about the striking of the autumn salmon: they have tough jaws, especially the cock fish; don't be afraid to set the hook firmly. But, unlike the smaller grilse of the summer months, which can take the fly with great speed from the swiftest of water, the heavy autumn salmon is much slower. It must be given time to turn away with the fly before the hook is set. A length of loose line held below the reel ensures that the strike is not too quick. An angler on the Tweed, who fishes with a 14-foot spliced green-heart and a reel with a strong check, allows his fish to take five to ten yards of line off the reel as it takes the fly. Only then does he strike. It is exciting to watch, but extremely difficult to do. It requires strong willpower, and not a little nerve — but he rarely misses a fish.

The autumn salmon is short and thick; it will weigh anything from 10 lb. to 25 lb. or more. It will not be long in the river; as the time for spawning draws near the urgent water compels it onward. The grilse of the summer months is now red, soft in the belly; it puts up a poor fight. It should be handled with loving care, and returned to the river with gentleness.

For many anglers, this is the time for the sunk

7. TO CHRISTEN A GREENHEART

I managed a day's fishing one autumn with a friend of mine on the Tweed. It was really an excuse to try out a fine spliced greenheart rod.

Paddy Avery had had the rod made for him by a local ghillie, and it had yet to be christened.

We started fishing from the boat around 2.30

in the afternoon. Conditions were far from perfect — little current in the pool, no wind, and a lot of weed held in position by the stump of a submerged tree. The boat drifted down on to the top end of the weed and held . . .

My first offering — a Stoat's Tail — produced nothing, and with so many fish obviously being covered, I quickly changed to a Yellow Dog tube about 1½ inches long.

I wasn't ready for the first fish as it snatched at the fly, and an excited strike produced nothing. A few casts later, and a steady pull on the fly, and I was into my first autumn fish this year. We quietly rowed the fish upstream and clear of the other salmon. After a ten-minute struggle, 14 lb. of fish was carefully tailed to the bank. Another followed — much the same as the first.

Not believing our luck from what, at first glance, was not productive water, I lengthened the cast to cover yet another likely head and tail. The line drew firmly, and this time, head shaking like a dog, the fish backed off downstream.

Twenty minutes later, and half the backing gone for the second time, I was beginning to wonder what size this salmon was, when it charged back upstream and straight into weed — the fly slipped on to the surface and the monster had gone!

The rod was royally christened that afternoon. In less than three hours we landed five fish, from 9 lb. to 14 lb. — not to mention the proverbial 'one that got away'.

I might have been unlucky losing my biggest fish of the day, but the tenant on the English side of the river hooked and lost an even bigger salmon in the morning. After forty minutes and some spectacular leaps, the fish broke free. Ghillie Alex Brown who has over 2,000 salmon to his own credit, reckoned the fish was upwards of 35 lb. It's typical of Tweed autumn fishing that you don't quite know when the really big fish will take. Some of the back end cock fish run well over 40 lb. and will smash all but the strongest gear.

After fishing for several years with a hollow glass rod, the change to the greenheart was spectacular — not the heavyweight 18-foot rods of twenty years ago, but a light 12-foot version which played fish as well as casting a fly. I'm converted, even if it takes longer to tape joints instead of the normal ferrules.

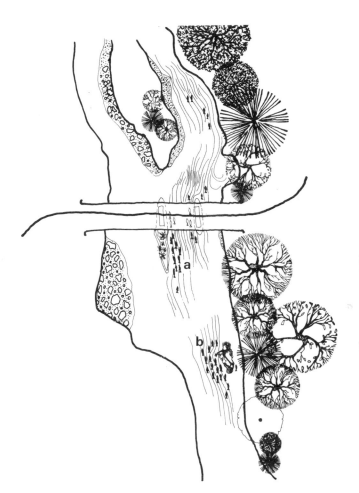

River Tweed at Norham Bridge. Fish lie under the main arch of the bridge; although difficult to approach with the fly, they are, however, catchable.

(a) Main taking lie below the bridge, often fished from the banking below the main arch, reached by boat.

(b) An unusually successful lie, not fished until recent years. The sunken tree constricts the flow, and diverts the stream to form an excellent lie, where fish hold in low water conditions. An ideal taking point in the later months during low water. The author with his host, Paddy Avery took five fish averaging 14 lb. one October afternoon from the lie on a small tube fly, during a hectic one-and-a-half-hour spell of 'mackerel fishing'.

8. THE ESTUARY AND ABOVE

There is a progression of sport during any salmon year from the cold early days of January with deeply fished lures, through the youth of spring and the warming rays of early sun, to summer grilse time, the sometimes static in-between days of early September, and those final rich autumn days of fierce cock fish and deep flanked 'grey-backs'. The foregoing notes have looked at my own personal diary of fishing at these times — not for one specific year, but a general pattern which has developed through the seasons.

There is another clearly defined progression in salmon fishing which is often forgotten — the movement of the fish from estuary waters, upstream through the river's physical variations; the salmon's attitude to the angler's lure not only changes with the time of year, water conditions and micro-climate, but in its relative environment and distance from the sea.

Let's look at a number of situations, not all from the same water, and the salmon's attitude to change and movement.

Most of our rivers, by the time they reach the sea, are broad, powerful and sometimes meandering. If industry has not dealt them a total death blow, then with good fortune, salmon will run there. With few barriers on lower reaches, apart from pollution by man, most fish move quickly through the estuary waters until they hit the first of the real pools. If there is little or no water in the river these fish will stay in the estuary for weeks, often moving into fresh water with each tide, and then dropping back again. It is at times like this that commercial estuary netting can be so devastating. The same fish may have to pass the nets a dozen or more times before it finally decides to run upstream proper.

You can be lucky on the tidal pools, and many such stretches offer cheap if not very rewarding salmon fishing. Once the salmon hit the lower pools, where a strong run at the head of the stream tempts them to rest, then they will be keener to accept a lure. Spring fish will seldom tarry here long, but will nevertheless take a bait freely, given the right conditions. The summer salmon will seek the well oxygenated streams, and will often be happy to lie in lower reaches for many weeks before attempting their spawning run to the upper reaches and tributaries.

On the lower Tweed, most spring fish move quickly upstream until they reach the pools around Kelso. The weir just above the Tweed's junction with Teviot holds many fish back in January and February when the bulk of the spring fish come through the lower reaches. With the right water conditions, and a kind 'early spring', the fishing is amongst the finest in the world. And yet a few miles farther downstream, on pools which can be rich indeed in the autumn months if the river is none too heavy, few, if any, springers will stop long enough to take a bait. If the water is low, and a hard frost halts the fish, then a deeply sunk bait, fished slowly across the known lies, will perhaps take an odd resting fish.

On a beat I fish at Norham, my best sport is expected in the autumn, and only then if we have little rain. Even in low water conditions, the fish move upstream (Tweed is a big river), and are happy to rest a while in these lower pools. It is beautiful fly fishing water, and since the best of the fishing is in September and October when fly only is the rule, this is just as well.

In the autumn of 1972 and 1973, 'we' were fortunate in having near drought conditions which held the fish in the lower pools. A little rain excited the fish enough to show an interest in our flies, but not so much that they shot upstream, leaving us fishless. The normally prolific Kelso beats had so little water and so few fish, that rods were taking fewer fish in a week than would normally result from a morning's sport.

The Lower Ladykirk Beat on the River Tweed

The main pool on the Lower Ladykirk Beat at Norham offers the angler a number of splendid opportunities.

The beat begins half-way down a rather uninteresting flat. Fish do lie hard to the left bank, but with little current to carry a fly, and a high, heavily-wooded bank, fishing for them is all but out of the question. It is at the end of this flat where the strength of the river gathers itself into one forceful stream round the south side of a large island that the finest fishable lies are.

Looking downstream, little or no water passes between the island and the left bank, even in spate conditions, and the water sweeps round to form a deep, gravelly stream which offers ideal 'lying up' conditions for running fish. Even in times of high water in the autumn, I have seen fish move to the head of the pool, stop for a minute or two, and then on through into the pool above. If you can put a fly on to the nose of a running fish as it hits the head of the pool, he invariably takes. A Jungle Cock Stoat's Tail tube took two sea-liced fish during the first hours of an October spate within minutes of each other, and after the anglers had watched the fish move quickly up the pool, showing as they did so.

At its best, and that means low to medium flow of water, the fishing in the stream can be superb. Edinburgh angler Ian Calcott took three fine fish all around the 15 lb. mark, on a well sunk Stoat tube. My own fish from the stream that day, a seventeen-pounder, took a Yellow Dog tube. I was fishing a sinking line, but an un-weighted fly. Ian suggested casting more square to the current, and mending the line to put the fly deeper and slower over the fish. He was on!

On these lower stretches which tend to fish best in low water conditions the angler has the problem often of weed, even on the stronger streams. Lower Tweed is no exception, and one of the best fish I've hooked in recent years came unstuck in weed after a half-hour-long tussle. I had managed to work the fish almost back to my feet, and had about seven feet of the cast above water. Even then, I couldn't put the fish on its side, and never even saw a flash to indicate the size. Its strength must have put it in well over the 20 lb. mark. Weed snagged the line as the fish worked up the bank, and back came the fly.

On the island stream, a hooked fish had to be kept clear of the main lie, so as not to disturb the pool, but neither could you pressurize the fish into your own bank too quickly, or the weed spelt danger. It was better to tire the fish out in the main stream, but down from the holding lies, and then quickly and firmly walk the fish back

Ladykirk FISHINGS on Lower Tweed at Norham. This is excellent back end water, providing there is not too much water, otherwise fish run quickly through.

(a) The head of the island stream produces fish for the first hundred yards, with most of the fish lying central or to the right hand side of the stream. Heavy weed beds in autumn months to the left bank create a hazard for rods attempting to beach fish from this bank. At the tail of the stream, few fish are taken.

(b) At the bottom end of the island is an excellent hole, with an eddy to the right bank. Salmon take the fly well here, and do so facing downstream in the reversed current at times. The author has seen salmon chasing dace at this point, and has subsequently landed a fish on a small silver spoon after unsuccessful attempts with the fly.

(c) Although the main stream curls across to the left bank here, most salmon run the right bank, and in low water conditions can be taken on small flies in the autumn months by wading well across to the English bank. The author's best fish from the beat, a twenty-four-pounder was taken from here on a small shrimp tube.

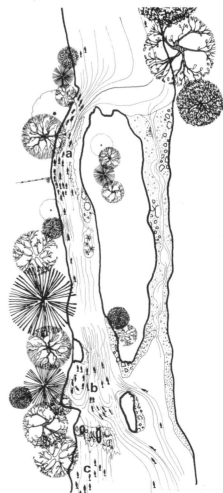

through the weed bank, keeping a steady pressure on the line. Without jerking, it is often possible to lead even a large fish in this manner — rather like taking a slow dog for a walk. You get the odd tug, but the fish will often move quite gently with you. Once clear of obstructions, heavier pressure generally produces a fireworks response from the fish.

At the tail of the island, there is another ideal fish station. In between, you can pick up the odd running fish, but luck would have to place your bait right on the fish for success.

On the English bank, across a heavy stream, the river curled back on itself in a splendid, shaded eddy. You are as likely to see a fish nose downstream as rise facing upriver. The trick is to place the fly at the top end of the backwater, rod held high to prevent the faster water whipping your fly, skating across the surface of the calmer water and out into the fast stream. A fish will seldom take a dragging fly, especially one breaking the surface, but it does happen.

A miscast across that very stream had made me decide to gather the line and replace the fly, and as I handlined in preparation for the backcast, a fish lunged at the fly. Unfortunately, he wouldn't come a second time, either to a conventionally placed fly, or to a dragged one.

There are plenty of coarse fish on Lower Tweed, and this particular stretch has shoals of fine dace, and the eddy in question generally holds a large shoal of these fish. On many occasions, I've seen several dace throw themselves into the air, chased by marauding trout or — as I think — salmon. Fish will often show. Head and tail porpoising antics generally indicate running fish, or takers. Running, skittering rises sideways across the pool are now known to indicate the presence of disease in many cases. A healthy jump can be caused by a fish fresh from the sea attempting perhaps to rid itself of sea lice, or maybe it's just high spirits. The fish I've watched in this particular eddy seem to play a game. You won't see a fish for a spell, and then several fish will throw themselves out of the water within seconds, and in all directions. Small silvery dace will then scatter, and up will come another salmon or two. I'm convinced that the salmon are attacking the dace, whether out of fun, or because of their natural feeding instincts, or perhaps they are just plain upset at having to share the lie with smaller shoal fish. (Miss Ballantyne's British record salmon from the Tay was taken on a dace, a bait which must have been collected from a border river or from England.)

My first experience on the Tweed of watching the salmon chasing the dace coincided with the last day of spinning for the year. Having fished carefully most of the day with the fly, including covering the dace-keen salmon with Silver Wilkinson, Silver Doctor, and other dace-like goodies, I decided to give them a last chance with a silver Toby spoon. First cast and the bait was hit hard as it fluttered round from the eddy into the main current. Imitation dace or not, the sea-liced 12 lb. hen fish had the spoon well to the back of the mouth, and that was even after tightening immediately on the fish in fast water the moment it took the lure. I wonder what a silver Polystickle would have produced on my trout rod?

As the water gathers speed at the tail of the island, the main stream crosses from the right bank to the left, curving round a smaller island. Most of the fish, however, work their way up the quieter water on the right bank from down below.

'You're wasting your time,' was my companion's last prediction as he lugged three good fish from the upper stream back up the hill to the car. But, I ask you, slack water or not, fish after fish was performing a delightful head and tail rise, perhaps fifteen different fish queuing up. Irresistible. Certainly the water was slacker here, but the fish were lying in 3 or 4 feet of water over a fine, gravelly bottom — at least they would see a fly.

The light had nearly gone, but I took off the sinking tip, and bigger tube fly, reduced the cast strength to 10 lb. nylon, and tied on a small Jungle Cock shrimp. To reach the fish, I had to move well across the river, and this I did as slowly and as gently as possible. I don't agree with the 'don't talk too noisily on the bank' brigade. Fish don't hear you as such. Cast a shadow, or make a vibration through stomping up and down the bank or wading too briskly, and you *will* frighten fish. Once in position, I waited for the top fish to show again.

The movement and tip of the dorsal could have been taken for a trout nymphing, but there was no mistaking it was a fish. The line pulled, and the slack held loosely below the reel drew. I raised the rod, and the fish pulled quietly but powerfully across and down. I began to walk the fish quietly away from the lie, and towards my own bank, away from the other fish. The best laid plans, however, come unstuck, and so did this fish.

What went wrong? I didn't have time to think, as the light was going, and I intended putting a fly over at least one more fish. My disbelieving partner returned to see what was keeping me.

Another tail! The fly would be swinging round just on his nose. That delicious anticipation, and then the magic draw of the line, ever so gently this time. Again the slack pulled through my fingers, and I delayed even longer to let the fish take the strain as the rod was raised in an easy movement. BANG! The water erupted and hopes of dealing with the fish quietly had to be forgotten as an obviously good cock fish decided to do 'his thing'.

It took twenty minutes of careful handling to work the fish back into a tailing position. Even then, the fish cogged against the pressure of the line, doing a lazy head and tail motion against the current rather than giving in, and showing a broad flank. Ian put one hand then another round the thick wrist of the tail, and with a calculated heave, 24 lb. of cock fish was safe ashore. The wee, now tattered shrimp, was held firmly in the scissors, dwarfed by the well developed kype typical of a mature autumn cock fish approaching spawning. A proud fish . . .

9. MIXED FISHING ON THE TAY

That other large east coast Scottish river, the Tay, has some of its cheapest salmon fishing just above the estuary at Perth. The stretch is in part tidal, and the harbour itself can take ships in the hundreds of tons class. Robert the Second in the year 1375 granted to the community of Perth the right to take fish from the river here.

My introduction to this fishing is still well remembered. I had arrived on the North Inch, a long flat stretch where luck was as important as the lure you fished. Few clean fish were taken, but on this particular day the first fish I saw hooked was as fresh as a whistle. One of the old locals had hooked the salmon on a spun bait, and after a surprisingly brief struggle the fish came in towards the bank. One of the 'gallery' waded briskly into the river, declaring he would land the fish. As he grabbed the line, I let out an involuntary yell to let go. As he tailed the fish, still holding the line with his other hand, he turned, made for the bank, and stated that he'd landed more salmon than I had had hot . . . the fish slipped from his grip. His other hand didn't give its hold on the fragile cast, and away went the bonniest springer I had seen.

I was at that time — many years ago — a relatively uncomplicated angler, whether after salmon or other fish. The following notes went into my diary. . . .

Mixed fishing on the Tay
It's not long after the start of the year that I make my first fishing trip . . . to the River Tay at Perth. Most of the salmon fishings on the Tay are strictly preserved, and are rented for large sums of money. A few hotels have their own water or can arrange for salmon fishing on the river. To fish on these exclusive reaches remains for me just a dream, but there is one stretch I can fish, and land salmon — the town water of Perth.

Until a few years ago, this was free, although tickets were issued to restrict numbers of anglers, thus preventing overcrowding, which so often occurs on many association waters, such as the Tweed at Peebles. Today, the small charge made covers the cost of issuing day tickets and, at that, must be the cheapest salmon fishing to be had in Britain.

You will find it most busy on Saturdays, but it can be very quiet through the week. Sundays in Scotland are out as far as migratory fish are concerned, although nobody complains if one fishes in the harbour for the coarse fish.

The Tay at Perth is very broad, and although there is a powerful current, it has the appearance of sluggish water, very smooth, and with no real pools. In consequence, a fish can be expected anywhere. I have had salmon follow me right in to the bank before taking. I remember one in particular. It was the first time I had fished the Tay, and after not many minutes casting, I had walloped my Blue and Silver devon sixty yards out across the river, and had started a slow recovery when a large bump appeared immediately behind the lure. At first I thought a bit of weed had caught hold of the devon, but the normal resistance and feel of the devon told me it was fishing properly. I realized it was a fish, but it wasn't until my devon had travelled forty yards after the fish had first bumped the surface, that it took — right at my feet — with a swirl that took my breath away. On the bank, it weighed 16 lb., but it was a kelt, that is, a salmon which is returning to the sea having completed its spawning. The law says you return them, and that is only fair. They have played their part in maintaining the runs of fresh salmon in the years ahead, and those that survive are well worthy of our respect.

The unfortunate drawback Perth town water has as a salmon stretch is that, above the main road bridge, the river being a long glide, it does not invite clean, fresh run fish to stay; even when the water is at its coldest, salmon run straight through to the middle reaches and farther. Below the bridge, however, there is broken water which smooths into a glide at the tail of the run, and in low water, such as at the start of last season, numbers of salmon are taken.

It is not suitable fly water, and most fish are taken spinning; devons, spoons and sprats, dyed and natural, account for sea trout as well as salmon. The whitling, those small grilse sea trout of $\frac{3}{4}$ lb. in weight provide most of the sport. You are extremely lucky if you get a fresh run spring salmon, but during the day it is not unusual to have half-a-dozen or more salmon kelts. These can provide surprisingly good sport since many are well recovered from their recent activities and put up a powerful show, although in general they are not quite so acrobatic as clean fish. Don't be misled by those who say you just reel them in and throw them back as quickly as possible. This is what does happen on more exclusive stretches where plenty of clean fish are to be had, and the kelt is a nuisance and a disappointment. Only a few times have I hooked kelts that allowed themselves to be reeled in: and it has been more than once that a spawned fish has given me a better tussle than clean fish.

For the beginner at salmon fishing, the kelt saves disappointment, and can prove a worthy opponent — but be warned: it is sometimes not easy to tell the difference between a spawned fish and a clean salmon. Generally, the kelt is thin, and the vent red and extended. Fins can also be ragged, and the body red coloured or a brassy silver. Those who don't spin, fish worm on paternoster or leger tackle. They catch sea trout and the odd kelt — and flounders, roach and perch! Although many miles from the sea, large numbers of resident flounders are taken on worm. They are very tasty too, fried whole in butter. Vast shoals of pound-plus roach move in the slack water of the main river, and in the harbour also. It is to the harbour one goes for the best of the perch, which at times feed furiously on the small roach fry. I have seen two-pounders come out of here.

As for the roach, you can catch upwards of fifty in a single day, even in the coldest weather that January can produce, when you have to break the ice to get your bait in, and are endlessly clearing the rod rings of ice. As for average weight, they are not as large as those in the River Tyne, but one angler I met, told of one roach of nearly 4 lb., taken on a worm from the main river just below the second bridge during an early season spate: 'I believe,' he said, 'it ended up as food for the angler's cat!'

10. SPORT FIT FOR KINGS

There are on every major salmon river those stretches which most of us can only dream of . . . those rich, fat, lower stretches where the fresh-run fish first rest, and see the angler's lure for the first, and often, only time.

Much of my own salmon fishing has taken

Fresh-run Spring Salmon (*Salmo Salar*)
(sea-lice still on flanks)

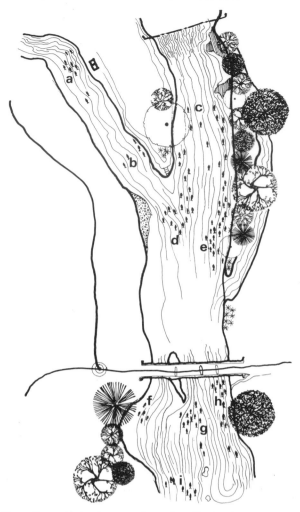

River Tweed; the famous Junction Pool where Teviot joins Tweed at Kelso.

(a) Jack's Plumb — produces excellent spring fishing, with most fish lying well up into the stream. In high water, this stretch fishes well right down to its junction with Tweed (b).
(c) Depending on river height, fish take well up the stream towards the weir.
(d) The 'Pot' gives excellent lies, and is a favourite taking spot.
(e) One of the ghillie's favourite taking lies, fish hold hard to the island, and can be taken the whole length of the stream.
(f) Fish lie in the slacker water here, and can take well in the spring and late autumn.
(g/h) Excellent fly water in the Bridge Pool, particularly in the streams flowing below the second and third arches.
(i) Excellent in a high water, with well sunk fly and spinning, during later months especially, Fishes well in the spring from the willows right down past the White Dyke to the weir at Hempseedford.

place on association water, and on cheaper stretches where the catch is invariably measured in a handful of fish for a whole season's hard fishing. Association water is excellent testing ground, and will teach you much about salmon and the difficulty of catching one.

The Kelso Junction Pool, Tweed

Just once in a while, I've been lucky to fish water the equal of any in Europe. One such stretch of water is the famous Junction Pool, where Teviot meets Tweed at Kelso.

This is a classic stream. Near to the estuary, fish are quickly up from salt water, and the weir at the head of the main pool is sufficient obstruction for spring and autumn fish to tarry.

It is the spring fishing which is so justly famous. By late April, the fish of the earlier months have all but moved through. While summer will produce some grilse, fishing can often be poor, and tickets are available locally for only a pound or two. This does, however, reflect the chances of sport. If a spate occurs, then fishing prospects in summer are immediately good, but you will be just one of several hundred eager locals wanting a ticket while the run is on.

The Duke of Roxburgh wisely and generously offers local anglers excellent salmon fishing on the Teviot a short distance above its junction with Tweed, and many fish are taken each year. The main Junction Pool includes several hundred yards of the lower Teviot, and it can produce good sport with springers and autumn fish on fly and spinning, especially when high water makes fishing in the main river difficult. It is in the main stream, however, that most of the anglers search for sea-liced fish.

Tweed springers are not large fish, perhaps averaging only 7 lb., but they are bold fighters and, given good conditions, this pool can yield upwards of twenty fish in a day.

I shared a rod there in February, in 1973 and 1974. The first time not enough water and cold, sunny conditions kept the fish down. We did have fish, but not to my own rod. In 1974, my afternoon on 'The Junction' produced nothing until 4.40 p.m., just as the sun dropped low in the sky. Strangely, though, the light was better than it had been all day, and the sun broke through the cloud to give that rich, low-angled light that promises a fish on an early spring day. A slowly fished hair-wing tube over the ghillie's favourite lie (c) met with response as a small 'springer' pulled the fly into the scissors of the jaw. We quickly beached the boat, and I was out waiting for the fish to respond with a bit more vigour. Nothing happened. A quick consultation, and the net was placed carefully into the water, and the fish drawn over its rim. Barely 6 lb., but fresh-run. Perhaps that was the trouble. I've never had a poor fight from a summer or autumn fish, and only occasionally from kelts, but springers can be a disappointment. Perhaps they are over-eager in their initial rush into fresh water. Perhaps the chemical change from salt water to fresh early in the year is too acute? Alan Scott, a fine Inverness angler, took the heaviest springer from the Moriston Estuary Beat in over twenty years, a thirty-pounder, on his opening visit in January, 1974. It was on the bank in a few minutes.

We kept our tired springer, and covered the lie again. This time, barely three casts later, the fish threw itself out of the water before the line had pulled tight, and then she was gone; a better fish, nearer 12 lb. It was the end of our fishing for the day.

On the Bridge Pool, below the old bridge at Kelso, the lies are not so well defined, and the angler unaccustomed to the beat needs the advice of a friend who knows the water, and this is often the ghillie.

Let's look at the various lies on this stretch of water, and see how outward indications can lead us to the fish.

(a) At the head of the first main stream on the Teviot a fly will produce a fresh fish. From here, down to the junction with Tweed, there are fish to be taken, but with an even current it is more difficult to pinpoint lying fish.

(b) Few fish will lie here, but when the run is on, fresh fish move into the river all the time, and a well presented bait in the right place at the right time will take a salmon. Closer to the bank, especially early in the year, and again in the autumn, it is not unusual to spot kelts or even diseased fish. Few clean fish here, though, and with such magnificent fishing on the main river, nobody really pays too much attention.

(c) Depending on the height of water, fish can be taken on fly or spun baits from either side of the stream. In a very high water, anglers will not start fishing much more than fifty yards above the junction, but during lower water fish can be taken almost as far up as the weir itself.

(d) The river deepens on the downstream edge of the sandbank at the mouth of the Teviot where the deposits brought down by the current over the years have built into a sandy ridge. On

Beautiful summer fly water on the Upper Oykel in Sutherland.

the edge, the fish lie resting before moving into the Teviot or farther upstream, following the right bank of the river. It is an excellent taking lie, but one which has generally to be fished from a boat.

(*e*) This lie is typical of many salmon rivers: a superb gravelly glide with enough carry for the fly, offers the angler a choice of boat or bank fishing, and the fish fan out towards the tail of the current and can be taken over a fairly wide holding point. It seems a shame to even consider spinning such perfect water and, given the right conditions, salmon sometimes take the fly like shoal mackerel!

Bridge Pool

(*f*) The lie is in deep undercut close to the bank, and fish don't hold long here. They will be eager to move on upstream after a short rest. In high water, they won't stop at all.

(*g*) Fish will hold here longer in the autumn, and again fish will be moving through fairly rapidly. Excellent fly water.

(*h*) Again, a temporary resting place, and a fly or bait presented at the right time and on the nose of the fish will generally produce a response.

The shallowing of the stream below these main lies develops into a strong eddy on the left bank, and fish move over to the edge of the stream under the right bank. It is a deeper lie, and fish do tend to 'hold up' longer. A well sunk fly early in the year or a slowly fished bait will give the angler most chance of success.

Almondmouth on the Tay

In many ways, the fine Almondmouth Pool on the River Tay, only a mile or two above Perth, is very similar to the Kelso situation. However, the restrictions which hold the fish are natural and not man-made. The river takes a sharp bend here, and with a shallow gravel bank running three-quarters of the way across from the right bank, most of the force of the current comes down the left bank. Where the gravel slopes away into the main pool, the fish nose their way hard up to the lip of the pool, where the depth suddenly changes from a matter of inches to three or four feet. Hang a fly carefully from a wading position above, and you're in business.

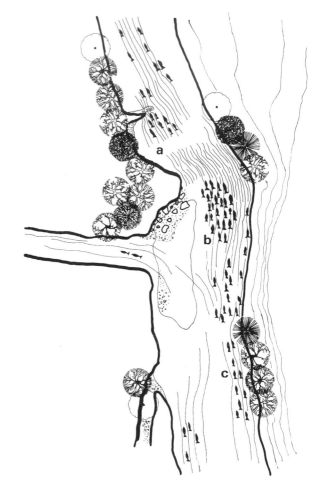

River Tay, Almondmouth.

With a strong flow running down the left bank, the fish lie at the head of the pool on the right-hand edge of the main current. Fishing from the far bank needs skill, and it is best fished by 'hanging' the bait over the fast water, to allow it to sink, and then fished as slowly as possible over the lie before being whisked away in the current.

24

Fish that are taken on the left bank (position c) and hard in to the bank are generally runners, but with fresh fish moving in on each tide, sport can be steady. Those close to the bank, however, don't tarry long, and most of the fish are taken from the head of the pool (b).

Those fish that eventually move through the stream, and that depend on water, move across to the right bank, and often lie in streamy water (a) behind some large rocks which break the current. As they move into the main pool above, they spread out, and can be taken anywhere across the breadth of the river.

Spring can be excellent, but too much water allows the fish to run through the main holding pool. A big water in the autumn means the same, but the fish at that time are moving upstream in such numbers that sport is virtually guaranteed. If the river is low, the shallow gravel bar can hold the fish in the stream for longer, and produces magnificent fly fishing.

The importance of getting a bait down in a lie where you are fishing over a strong stream cannot be stressed enough. A bait fishing too quickly over the lie and too high in the water will be ignored. Once you have hooked your fish in a situation like this, the salmon will without fail move straight into the fast water, and you have to be prepared to head downstream at speed after the 'catch'. If you have hooked your fish over a fast stream into slack water, the odds are that you are on the high bank, no doubt with its very own selection of shrubs and trees. This is known as fishing the hard way, and if you are unaccompanied, the problems involved in landing the fish are difficult to overcome.

How do you land a fish? The water will not only be fast right at your feet, but also deep. Hand-tailing a fish in these circumstances is not only risky, but could be dangerous. A mechanical tailer is perhaps better, although I normally avoid the things (you're liable to lasso anything within striking distance apart from the fish). Gaffs I don't like, although they can be efficient. I've seen wounded fish come off the gaff and break the line, and I'd rather see a fish escape with a chance of survival, if it is able to throw the hook. Perhaps it's through seeing too much sea angling and the misuse of gaffs that has put me off them. In spring they are better left at home because of the number of kelts about which, well-mended, can look surprisingly like fresh-run springers straight up from the sea.

That leaves a net which, if you have the strength to wield one big enough, is perhaps the best way of all. Never 'slash' at a fish with the net. Have it in place below the water line before *drawing the fish over the net*, and *not* the other way round, by sliding the net under the fish. Too much movement, and your fish will be away.

The lower beats on any river offer the angler an opportunity to see a variety of fish fresh in from the sea, often carrying the rigours of their endurance through the estuary and tidal waters. Once upstream, the signs disappear, and wounds heal.

Out of four spring fish taken in February in one morning's fishing at Kelso at the start of the 1974 season, two had been attacked by estuary seals within hours of being caught. Fish A had a lucky escape. The seal's webbed claw had only just grazed the skin, and removed some of the scales. I wondered, looking at that fish, how much the seal was playing, or sporting with the salmon, and how much was he really intent on feeding?

It's rather like trying to guess why a salmon takes a bait. Most suggestions are plausible, and they are all equally correct at different times. Fish will take a bait in fresh water, although incapable of feeding, through instinct, memory of sea feeding, frustration or annoyance, teasing, aggression, and even for fun. I'm sure in the autumn many fish are declaring a territorial right, and take a fly to be an intruding parr (parr are known to be sexually mature, and capable of fertilizing the hen fish's eggs). On the Tay and Tweed where I do most of my autumn fishing, the percentage of cocks to hens taken is about four to one, and the fish leave you in no doubt as to the forcefulness of the take, compared to the gentle summer grilse.

As yet, I have not read or heard of any salmon angler adding another very simple explanation as to why fish will take a bait. A salmon sees an object floating, swimming, fluttering or spinning past his nose. He's interested, but is not necessarily thinking about food. He wants to stop 'it'. Oops, no hands! Simple, the fish has to use its mouth, for no other reason than it is the only way that the fish can stop the object of his curiosity. Taking this thought a bit further, the occasional foul-hooked fish taken while greased-lining, is not necessarily the result of mistiming on the 'strike'. There are many predators in the sea which use their tails or bodies to stun smaller shoal fish, and then eat them at their leisure. How much easier for a salmon to batter through a shoal of herring, stun a dozen or more, and then feed. Certainly easier than pinpointing a single fish. A playful swipe or roll over your fly could be no more than a playful 'strike' at an interesting object, with no chance of the bait ever being taken in the mouth.

I enjoy fishing worm for salmon — my love for sea fishing again no doubt — and in summer and autumn it can be a deadly way of taking fish. I don't see any problem in explaining why a fish should take a bunch of worms when it doesn't feed in fresh water; they wriggle, they swim close to the bottom where the fish are, and they move slower than a fly or lure. I'm sure they're also great fun to 'handle' with the mouth — if you're a non-feeding salmon that is!

Fish B — the second victim of a seal — wasn't so lucky. A deep wound caused by a hungry seal could have finished the long journey abruptly. The delight of a new season on the banks of one of the finest salmon rivers in the world couldn't entirely obliterate the thought of how vulnerable salmon are — at every turn they have to fight for their life. There were other fish that missed our flies. They would perhaps be taken upstream by other lucky anglers, or an otter might feed her young with fresh salmon instead of eels. Worse fate: the poacher's net, gaff or criminal cyanide might take life. Then, even worse, human forms of pollution — from industry, abstraction or effluent — add their toll. And at the end of the journey, there is furunculosis, or ulcerative dermal necrosis or kelt exhaustion. Who'd be a salmon?

II. A TALE OF TWO SALMON

Scottish anglers are very touchy about game fishing, and salmon in particular. Understandably, with so much fine game fishing available, the humble roach and pike play second fiddle to their adipose friends the trout and salmon. In spite of the excellent quality and quantity of both of these fish in our northern waters it seems a pity that coarse and game fish should live together in a relatively happy state when the same thing rarely applies to their respective captors. The conflict of interest which so many maintain seldom really exists.

I admit to having been personally rather vexed to find a number of rods one morning on a favourite salmon pool on lower Tweed. All were fishing bait on the far bank in late October amidst large numbers of salmon and sea trout which were running upstream to spawn. It became even more embarrassing when one of the anglers hooked and skilfully landed a $2\frac{1}{2}$ lb. sea trout from under my nose. He asked politely whether he was allowed to keep the fish. Since the salmon tenant on the English side hadn't turned up, I saw no reason for him not to keep the fish and told him so. He was absolutely

thrilled. My 'generosity' must have been noted by that 'Greatest of Fishers' for on my very next cast, the fly produced that delicious response of a drawing line and the battling fury of a sea-liced bar of silver straight from the sea. On the bank it weighed $16\frac{1}{2}$ lb. I hadn't to say a word to my fellow anglers on the far bank. To a man they all immediately stopped fishing when I hooked the salmon and were obviously enjoying the battle royal as surely as if they had been on the playing end themselves. It's a pity that we can't always be as tolerant of each other's fishing interests.

I well remember on one occasion fishing the dusk for salmon on the River Annan with a distinguished Scottish game fisher several years ago. There were few fish on our particular beat at Hoddom and my partner had perhaps wisely quitted the salmon rod for his lighter trout gear and a cast of sea trout flies. His first fish of the evening turned out to be a chub which had sucked his bob fly from the surface as it landed deftly underneath a bush on the far bank. The second fish followed shortly afterwards in the gloaming and immediately splashed on the surface. 'Another bloody chub,' came the curses from below me, as the angler unceremoniously waded back out of the pool mercilessly dragging the fish across the water and on to the gravel. Had it been lighter, the look on his face could well have been recorded for eternity. At his feet lay the most beautifully proportioned sea trout that I have seen; and it hadn't had a chance!

My 'Tale of two Salmon' really concerns two other Scottish waters, the Tay and the Teith.

Friend Jim was a novice angler, chasing that elusive first 'fish'. It was autumn on an attractive stretch of the Tay — not one of those prolific beats, but good fishing, especially at the tail end of the year. 'Look out for the "Sticks" and "Poos"' had been my instructions from an angling mate who had successfully fished the beat the previous weekend.

In our eagerness to arrive by the water in plenty of time, we were out of the car, across two fields and on the river bank assembling rods before the sun was up. I could sense a figure moving quietly but quickly across the field in the half light towards us. It was the keeper, accompanied by his dog, and a strong stick.

'Eh . . . Mr. Shepley?' enquired a Perthshire voice. 'Well, that's fine enough, I wasn't sure; I heard the car, and thought it could have been poachers. The two gates behind you to the main road are locked, and I left word to ring the police if I was a while getting back.'

Heaven help the poachers!

Our visitor proved to be extremely helpful in pointing the main lies in the two pools available, and even before full light, the number of splashing fish gave us a thrill of anticipated sport. I invited the keeper to join us later, and the reply was one of delight, and the word that he would pop down for the last half hour of the day as he had other work to do.

'Mind the fish just upstream from the "sticks",' he said as he turned back for the field, waving in the direction of a fallen tree, half submerged in the water. 'And up yonder close to the bank, that's where the "poos" are generally.' I suddenly had visions of small 'Winnie' type creatures, or even Tolkein 'hobbits' stalking the banks.

I cast my spoon across to the far bank, and allowed the current to work the bait unaided back across the stream. Second cast, and the bait nudged the far bank, and plopped quietly into the water. The line drew, and he was on.

'There's a "poo", and you have him!' came a

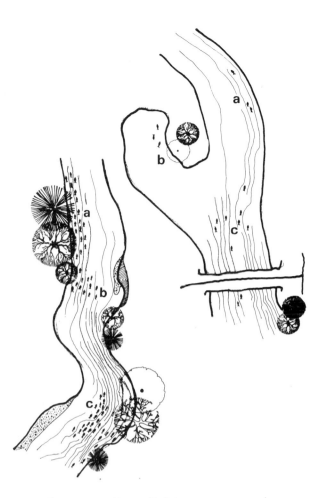

Left: River Tay at Upper Delvine.

(a) The 'poos', where a well placed bait hard to the right bank generally meant a firm take from salmon during the autumn months.
(b) The 'sticks', where on a day when the river was full of salmon, one rod took a sea trout, and even more surprisingly a pike!
(c) Fish lie on the far side of the stream, and anglers fishing from the left bank have to 'hang' the bait slowly over the lie. It was here that the monstrous autumn fish was lost after a brief struggle.

Right: River Teith at Callander.

(a) Chance of fish in the spring and autumn. The river runs too slowly here for summer fish. It was on this slow stretch that the pike was taken.
(b) Summer salmon which have been in the water some time generally sport themselves in the horse-shoe bay, but remain virtually uncatchable.
(c) One or two fish lie in the stream above and below the bridge, but require skill and a quiet approach if they are to be fooled.

satisfied voice from the middle distance behind me. 'Just where I said.'

An eight-pounder at ten minutes to eight on an October morning is no mean start to a day.

Jim was given the chance of his first salmon down at the 'sticks'. I'd moved on to the lower stream when there was a shout, 'FISH!' I ran up the bank, delighted that another salmon angler was about to be christened.

The fish tired quickly, and I moved into the water quietly and waited for a chance to tail the fish. The barred dorsal fin well back towards the tail of the slim green body was a complete surprise. A pike from a river full of salmon! I didn't believe it until *Esox* was on the bank — a well-fed eight-pounder.

The Tay is not noted for pike, but I've since learnt over the years that they are more plentiful than most anglers would like, or realize. There have been other pike which have fallen to a salmon bait, including fish which wouldn't disgrace a Norfolk Broads specimen hunter. One pike came to my own rod on an unproductive February day at Logierait when I plopped a silver sprat under some trees in a backwater which I had remarked to my companion as being 'extremely pikey'. It didn't stop me getting that snatch of excitement as a pike unexpectedly smashed into the bait right at my feet.

The River Teith, a major tributary of the Forth, is a lesser salmon water, but worthy of a visit. Many years ago, Jimmy Bain the local tackle dealer, who has since retired, told me I must be mistaken about seeing a pike in the river. The next day, a Sunday (and that means no salmon fishing in Scotland) I took a walk along the bank and found my finny friend chasing minnows . . . without a great deal of success.

Some bread and a jam jar, and I was soon fishing for minnows. A quick flick to kill one or two, and I was able to study at close quarters a jack pike feeding. He would lie perfectly still, in the shade of the bank. The first minnow I popped in, fluttered down to the bottom, right in front of his nose. He turned slightly, but didn't react. The next minnow fluttered down, the pike turned and lined up for attack, and then with surprising speed, hit the minnow from the side. A gulp, and it was gone. I returned the following day and caught the greedy pike; in the case of a game fishery, it was better out of this particular water anyway. My tackle dealer was convinced.

What he still doesn't know (that is until now) is that the double figure pike I brought in again the next day in my best schoolboy prank manner — well I was only fourteen — came not from the River Teith, but half-an-hour's bicycle ride over the hill at the Lake of Menteith. The Lake in those days was full of pike and perch, and some big trout. It had formerly been a trout fishery of note which had eventually reverted back to coarse fish. Today, under the management of Bobby Nisbet, it offers locals and visitors excellent brown and rainbow trout. Perhaps my Teith 'salmon' was one step towards the return of the fly rod to the Lake.

12. AN HISTORIC ISLAND - CAPUTH BRIDGE ON THE TAY

Miss G. W. Ballantyne's record fish of 64 lb. was taken from the River Tay fifty years ago. It came from a stretch of the river upstream of the village of Caputh, and after a long struggle was eventually beached on the island below Caputh Bridge. I have landed lesser salmon from the same island, and each time, experienced the thrill of sharing a little part of history, in my mind's eye, seeing that great salmon safely ashore. What a fish it must have been.

Since those days, the salmon which run our rivers in Europe have had less chance of survival. Commercial fishing, disease and pollution take a major toll; and yet the big fish of the Tay still run. Every year, fish in the 40-lb. class are taken, and in recent seasons one fine cock fish came within

Salmon Parr (*Salmo Salar*) (young salmon)

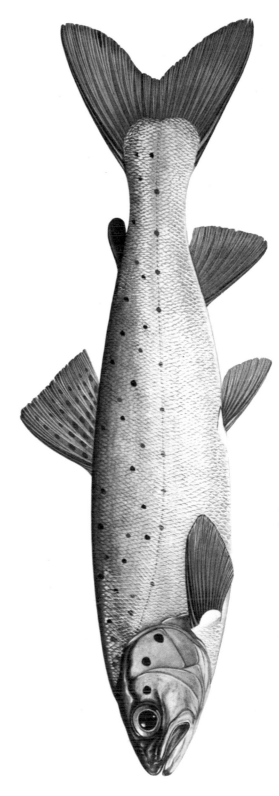

Salmon Smolt (*Salmo Salar*) later stage of above

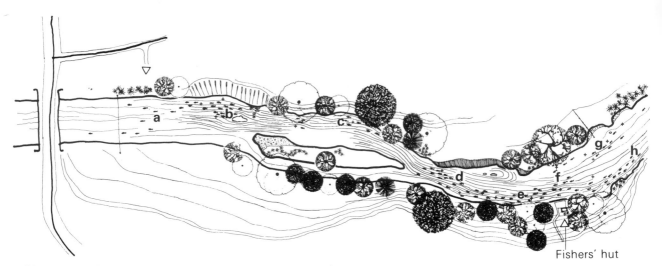

Fishers' hut

River Tay at Caputh.

(a) Salmon can be anywhere across the stream, and are generally running fish.

(b) The main taking lie. Fish rest here having run through from the stream below.

(c) Fish resting briefly under the trees can be taken on the fly in the summer and early autumn. The island is where Miss G. W. Ballantyne landed her British Record salmon.

(d/e) Fish take well in this stream, and the heavy water at the head of this pool invites fish to rest on the edge of the stream. Good fly water as well as spinning in spring and autumn.

(f) Fish spread out across the river, and can be picked up from main lies directly opposite the fishing hut on the right bank.

(g/h) Depending on the bank, fish can be taken mainly on spun lures or natural baits. Good autumn water and early spring. Insufficient current for summer salmon which lie well up the stream.

---

10 lb. of the age-long record. I've seen a forty-four-pounder from Kinnaird which dwarfed a summer grilse taken on the same day. It was the best Scottish salmon in 1972. Callum Gillies, is the ghillie on Kinnaird, and ensured that Bernard Blomefield who took the fish was in the right place at the right time, and then safely landed the salmon. Callum's guest on an eventful day in 1973 took the Tay's best of the year, a forty-two-pounder, just one of several fish in that bracket taken in the autumn.

There are mighty fish lost as well, and although I've never hooked one of these monsters myself, I witnessed a fish hooked and played for only minutes which, having cleared the water three times, took off for the sea. The angler, on a difficult bank, and unable to follow because of trees watched the line slipping off the reel until the spool emptied, and the fish was gone. The keeper would not estimate the weight of the enormous cock fish, but put it in a different category from a thirty-five-pounder taken from the same pool a couple of days previously. Perhaps I haven't seen enough big salmon to judge, but this fish was far closer to fifty pounds than forty-nine!

The pools below Caputh have produced their share of big fish. The best spring fish in March was a fine thirty-eight-pounder taken spinning a few years ago.

The beat begins where telegraph lines cross the top pool, which is more of a long flat. With few features this part of the river (*a*) can produce occasional fish, but the angler never knows exactly where a lying fish is.

A little farther down towards the tail (*b*), the water quickens and comes across to the left bank, forced over by the shallowing shingle at the start of the island. The lie is an excellent taking spot, with fish resting there for quite some time after negotiating the heavy water below. Even in the lowest summer water, this stream offers an opportunity of fish. Bill Currie, who fished the beat, often referred to the stream as a 'river within a river'. The character of the Tay changes as with all rivers, depending on the water height. Its transformation, however, is not from a fishable river to a tap-like trickle with stagnant ponds between, as with so many waters. A whole new environment, offering the fish a choice of lies, and the angler a series of fishing situations is unfolded as the river drops back and bares its structure. The Tay is a multi-dimensional water, adaptable at all times and, what is even more important, a new experience on every visit.

Between the two main pools (*c*), fish lie up in the shallow stream in the shade of summer trees, and a small fly can produce exciting sport. The main stream (*d*) offers the angler the chance of fish throughout the season, and we frequently took the first springers of a cold January on the fly well up towards the head of the stream from the farm bank (*left*). A well placed fly in the stream would also produce pulls from small well-mended kelts, generally cock fish.

Down at the fishing hut (*f*), there would always be the chance of a clean fish, most unfortunately rather inaccessible except with a spun lure. Any fly fisherman who has mastered the roll or 'Spey' cast would no doubt stand the chance of a fly-caught fish from this wooded bank. This allows the fly to be 'rolled out' by switching the rod without the main line totally leaving the water. With obstructions on the bank such as overhead trees and a steep banking, it allows the competent angler to push his fly well out over the stream. The fast water (*e*) immediately above the main lie will produce the chance of a running fish.

As the stream spreads into the 'belly' of the pool, the fish split, and tend to lie either side of the river (*g* and *h*). With such a wide river at this point, it depends on which bank the angler fishes which group of salmon are worthy of attention. The choice then becomes one of light, and on this particular pool the right bank, being very high, keeps the sun off the water apart from an hour or so at mid-day. Afternoons are generally reserved for the left bank, therefore, and the method appears to work well enough. With anglers fishing both banks for most of the day, it is interesting just how consistent has been the change of sport from morning activity on the right bank to sport for the other bank in the afternoon. I don't think the situation is unique.

13. ASSOCIATION WATER

You will see in some Scottish guide books to salmon fishing with reference to the famous river, the Tweed, that association water around Peebles and Innerleithen can fish very well in February. Perhaps the writer was also a kelt addict but the inference to someone who doesn't know the Tweed is that he has a reasonable chance of a clean fish and this is not the case. Spring salmon on the Tweed are small, generally averaging around the 7—8 lb. mark and seldom are they taken farther upstream than Galashiels until the season is well under way and, indeed, the bulk of the sport centres mainly around the fat lower stretches near Kelso.

The famous Junction Pool where the Teviot joins Tweed just above Kelso bridge is probably one of Europe's most famous pools and on its day can produce spectacular sport with fresh-run fish. The association water upstream has to wait longer, however, before the rods have a chance of spring sport and rarely are fish taken even as early as March. My first springer ever came from the Neidpath Castle Pool on the Tweed just above Peebles. It was an 8½-lb. cock fish which fell to a small toby spoon on 26 March and was such an unusual catch for the time of year that as a youngster I rushed back to the local tackle shop where it was proudly displayed hanging up outside the shop for all to see.

There is a strange situation on the River Tweed whereby anglers have to fish fly only for the first fortnight from 1 February until the commercial salmon nets come on, on 15 February. This results in anglers generally having to fish very large flies with heavy rods to throw them. One not so daft Irish friend of mine, who drives a motor bike, even goes as far as to keep his helmet on while fishing these big tubes in the early spring to save rather painful bruising if the cast is mis-timed and the fly belts you on the back of the head. Anyone who has experienced this would agree that the force from such a small object is quite alarming.

A favourite bait of mine in the early months on

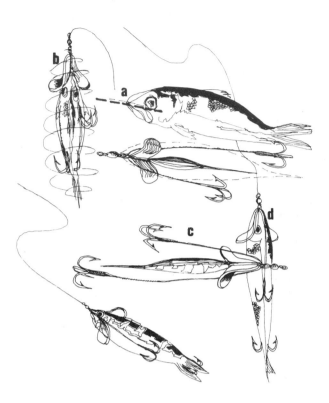

Sprat Mount.

(a) Few anglers bother to present a sprat properly on a spinning mount. One of the first things to do is to slit the head of the bait lengthways with a sharp razor blade, back to the gill cover: this allows the natural bait to slide up the mount, and past the plastic fins. The head can be secured at the swivel with elastic thread wound back down the length of the body.

(b) The effect of a badly mounted bait, where the sprat is slipped up the mount to the back side of the spinning fins. The brass mount and swivel which support the fins now protrude at least an inch beyond the sprat, and in the water the lure gives the impression of a 'mini-swordfish'.

(c) The shorter hook mount is generally fitted with a treble hook with one of the points angled to fit snugly into the sprat and hold it in place.

(d) A properly mounted bait, with the mouth of the sprat immediately behind the swivel. Not only will the bait look more lifelike and 'swim' better, but the sprat will last on the mount far longer than a hurriedly produced bait.

any river is the sprat and the only complaint is when there are a large number of kelts about, they seem to hit the sprat at every opportunity and a lot of time can be spent mounting up a fresh bait. The answer, of course, is to mount several baits before you start but even then time can be lost in preparing further lures. Most anglers mount the sprat on a spinning tackle with little thought to the final appearance of the bait. Generally, with clear perspex veins and a brass mount, the completed bait gives the impression of a small swordfish with the top end of the mound protruding from the mouth of the sprat. My preference is to split the sprat lengthways with a razor blade to the back of the gill case, so that top and bottom sections can be slid over the front of the mount and then secured with elastic cotton. The final bait gives the impression of a nice, fat round fish and there are no loose ends to spoil the action in the water. The sprat is a particularly favourite bait in the spring because of its relatively slow action — much the same as that of a wooden devon — and no matter how fast the bait is retrieved, the spin itself always has the appearance of a flutter rather than the hard mechanical movement of a metal devon. Perhaps for this reason too, wooden devons and the favourite Scottish bait, the Yellow Belly, are so successful in spring fishing conditions. At any time, of course, the wooden devon with a barrel lead farther up the cast has a much more attractive action following the contours of the river bottom than a metal bait.

Discipline and politeness are all important on association water. With the number of interested sportsmen, fishing water these days is at a premium, and at the best times of the year this can mean queuing on the more popular pools. Never mind if you are not first down the pool. Often, I agree, the first rod of the day has a more than good chance of contacting a fish. But there is something to be said for being somewhat later in the queue, providing that the fish are not unsettled by noisy, irresponsible wading or the pseudo-fishing techniques of the autumn association water 'drag it across their backs' brigade. A fish may be slow to move, even to the extent of ignoring the first offerings. You come down the pool with a fresh approach — perhaps a smaller fly — perhaps it fishes round slower than the last and at a different depth. Bang, you're into a fish!

A close friend of mine from Orkney is fishing daft. He also happens to be a commercial lobster

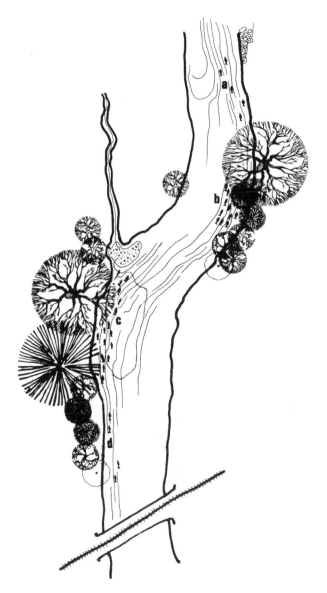

River Tweed, Association water, Peebleshire; the Cardrona Stretch (below).

(a) Surprisingly good lie often missed by other rods and consequently worth fishing. Apart from early season kelts, this water rarely produces fish until mid-September. Most of the fish are taken during the autumn months of October and November.
(b/c) Are the main lines.
(d) High water lies only.

Association water on the River Tweed (above).

(a) Fish lie hard to the steep rocky right bank, but can be fished from both banks. An autumn pool, where a well sunk fly fished slowly over the lie brings most success.

The large eddying pool on the corner the 'Dirt Pot' gives good autumn fly fishing in the main stream, and again towards the tail. If there is sufficient water in early September, the pool is sometimes carrying salmon which will take a spun bait. Little here at the start of the year apart from kelts.

Springers show a preference from late April onwards of lying in the pool below (b) the 'Nutwood'. They lie well over to the right bank at the head of the stream, or well over to the left bank under the trees farther downstream.

33

fisher. Now, Orkney lobsters are not as plentiful as they used to be — something to do with the popularity of the shellfish, and its value on a London plate and on the Continent. What did he do? The answer which produced an immediate improvement in the catch was deceptively simple. Every lobster boat working the grounds was fishing with the same size of creel, with the same size of opening for the lobsters to get at the bait. Bigger creels, with outsize funnels to lead the lobsters into the bait still caught the usual 'harvest' lobsters, but it also produced lobsters far too big for the traditional creels — monsters weighing six or more pounds. Here was a harvest which was totally untouched in heavily fished waters.

Where's the connection with salmon fishing?

On a highland east coast river, demand when the salmon are running means heavily fished water on the association water in question. From first light to dusk the pools are lined with rods intent on taking a fish. Take your dog for a walk on the river bank after dark and, apart from a handful of fly rods fishing for night sea trout, you wouldn't expect to see anyone salmon fishing — or would you? We all know salmon don't take

a bait after dark, just as surely as salmon don't take in salt water. Someone should have told this to those salmon taken off the east coast of Canada. There are other Atlantic salmon taken in the sea regularly on rod off the Mayo Coastline in Ireland. Any Orcadian will show the visitor the best marks for worming for a 'fish' in the sea, and they mean salmon!

I've rarely tried for salmon at night, mainly because it's something which is not generally accepted by the salmon angler. Certainly, there have been occasional night-time salmon taken by chance on highland rivers while after sea trout, but only where stocks have been high. Try your summer association water after dark with the fly; you could be surprised. Three salmon in one night from heavily fished association water is a good catch in anyone's log book. The fly in question was a No. 8 low-water hook — a few wisps of white hair, and a brilliant fluorescent orange body. The inventor was of the opinion that the white hair did the trick and not the body colour. There's no doubt that a White Wing is often successful for summer and autumn fish just as the light begins to fail. Next time out, I'm going to give the 'gloaming' a closer look.

14. THE HOTEL BEAT

In between the hard-fished association waters, and the rich man's exclusive beat on most salmon rivers, there is the hotel water. Remarkably good salmon fishing can still be obtained from many hotels for a pound or two per day. The overall cost of your fishing is generally a reasonable indication of the chances of sport, but there are exceptions.

One favourite beat of mine is the Church Pool on the Grantully Castle water, available through the Logierait Hotels. The owner, Jim McFarlane, is an expert with the rod and gun, and understands well enough the odd hours and eccentricities of the dedicated salmon fisher. He also knows the river, and that includes the stretch that flows past his back door.

As you come over the hill and down through

the woods, the Church Pool is a dream of a place. I've often drawn a blank, as far as the fish are concerned, but never in terms of the wealth of pleasure derived from being in a perfect place. The top pools (a, b) have produced January kelts in a howling blizzard. Even since the advent of UDN, one early day produced two late afternoon kelts (a) on a natural sprat from shallow water. That was a small triumph since nobody had even touched a fish all day. The water was low, and very clear. The odd kelt splashing about would not look at a fly or spun bait. A small devon looked exactly what it was — a spinning piece of metal. The fluttering sprat which curled round in the current could have been alive, and I watched the fish turn and take the bait without hesitation. Success.

In August, it was more like swimming-trunk weather. Some experts in the art (I mean it) of prawning, had been fishing steadily on the main stream all morning. Prawn, worm, spoon, devon, you name it. The fish, what few there were wouldn't be tempted.

After all that effort over the main holding lies, I didn't see much point in covering the same ground. I tied on a trout optic and moved into the fast water at the throat of the pool (c). The fly was taken by a large, stale fish on the first cast. I couldn't get back to the bank in time, and the fish had me on to the backing at speed. Back came the hook, twisted almost straight. It wasn't really the fault of the fine wire hook, it wasn't even meant for salmon. My mistake had been in continuing to fish a tiny fly on light nylon *on the salmon fly rod*. A light trout rod and reel would have matched the scale of the terminal tackle, and although giving me less power to play with, would have avoided the inevitable strain on the fly caused by the heavy gear.

In the autumn, the pool has been kind. Fish lie well down towards the tail (d), and can be taken successfully from either bank. One or two venture farther up under the trees (e), and require a deeply fished bait for most success. My favourite autumn sport, however, comes from the very tail of the pool (g) where the water picks up speed to sweep down the rapids which gurgle over boulders for three-quarters of a mile downstream.

You have to walk a hooked fish gently back up the left bank here, play it down to the tail of the pool, and then repeat the process until the fish tires. One false move, too much pressure at the wrong time, and the fish will be over the lip of the pool and into the fast water. Don't bother to follow it unless you can either swim or negotiate a slalom course without your own canoe. If you haven't brought a canoe along, there is no shortage of these craft during the summer months on either the Tweed or Tay. Saturday is a popular time for target practice. Seems a pity that a compromise can't be reached which would give weekend anglers peace on Saturday, and the canoeists can 'do their thing' on Sundays when salmon are protected by law.

The Church Pool, Grantully Castle Water, River Tay. An excellent all-season pool, which can produce some exceptional autumn sport.

(a) Fish lie here in cold water conditions in January and February.
(b) Fish move through this slow water fairly quickly, but can be taken at times spinning from the left bank.
(c) One of the main lies, this stream will fish right through the summer, and produced one August fish in bright sunshine on a trout fly fished by the author.
(d) Another good lie in streamy water.
(e) A quieter backwater, but one which produces fish on spun lures and natural bait throughout the year.
(f/g) Fish lie here after running through the fast water. Excellent taking place especially in the autumn.
(g) Is particularly good on a high water.

15. WHERE LOCH BECOMES RIVER

Once salmon arrive in a loch on their upstream journey, their distribution is something of a mystery. There are relatively few outward signs of where the fish run through a loch. The visitor needs more than at any other time the knowledge of the locals, and a couple of pints in the nearest hostelry with a successful salmon angler from the district is worth several days on a featureless stretch of water. Besides, most fishers, myself included, enjoy a beer and natter on things piscatorial; it's part of what fishing is about. The personal pleasure of sport is always enriched by the sharing of ideas with other anglers.

At Kenmore, Loch Tay gathers momentum and spills through the gap at Kenmore Bridge to form the first pools of the upper river. Most salmon fishers here head by boat into the 'guts' of the loch, to troll away the day with Kynoch Killer or sprat bait, in search of salmon unobserved. It is not a sport which I particularly enjoy. Trolling can be tedious, and unproductive for long spells.

Since I didn't have the local knowledge of the main salmon runs in the loch, my best bet was to restrict my attention to the tail of the loch, where one or two fresh fish were showing as they came through from the river. Once through the rapids they don't wait in the narrows of the loch, but push through to their favourite lies.

Most new fish show as they come through the bridge and then they are off. I was lucky to be in the right place as one such fish showed, and an accurately placed devon hit him on the nose and, bang, it was accepted.

A similar situation occurred from time to time on Loch Ailsh at the top of the Oykel River but, in this case, salmon hooked immediately above the start of the river were generally too taken on sea-trout flies intended for other fish.

The main holding point (as at Kenmore) was in the edge of the fast stream immediately below the outfall. Fish seemed to sense the loch ahead and would rest before making the final spirited burst into the calm of still water. Once they hit the loch they quickly moved up to the head of the loch, where the 'Upper Upper Oykel', the main spawning river, beckoned them to a September gathering.

Given rain, the Oykel could change from a roaring, peat-stained spate to ideal conditions of a clearing water in a matter of hours. In the space of a few days, the river could rise and fall several times, with predictable results. The first hour or two of a rise, would have the immediate response of fish homing to the fly. Thereafter, the fish would go off the take, no doubt more intent on making their way upstream. I also hold the opinion that in highland waters, the acidity of peat water off the grouse moors can 'sicken' the fish and put them down.

All the pools immediately below Loch Ailsh offer excellent fly water. My own favourites are the 'Black Bank' (b), where fish lie hard under the overhanging left peaty bank (hence the name), and the dubb farther down stream (d) formed by two outcrops of rock. The tail end of the main pool (c) with its curling eddy on the right bank could produce a delicious response at times by hanging the fly over the main current. Salmon would take a low water fly almost in the manner of a trout bumping a nymph.

I frequently fished a dropper on the Oykel, a practice not recommended by many salmon anglers of note. Admittedly, there are dangers in snagging dropper or tail fly during the fight, but the technique allows a pool to be covered with more than one size of fly and choice of pattern.

I even managed a 'classic double' when a sea trout and salmon took flies at the same time. A grilse had pulled at the single hair wing dropper, and as it set across the pool, a sea trout splashed wildly at the dragging tail tube — and connected. On a light fly rod scrambling over boulders and chasing a brace of fish down spate filled torrents, is exhilarating exercise to say the least.

Just how unpredictable fish can be was well illustrated by a fish from the pot below the main

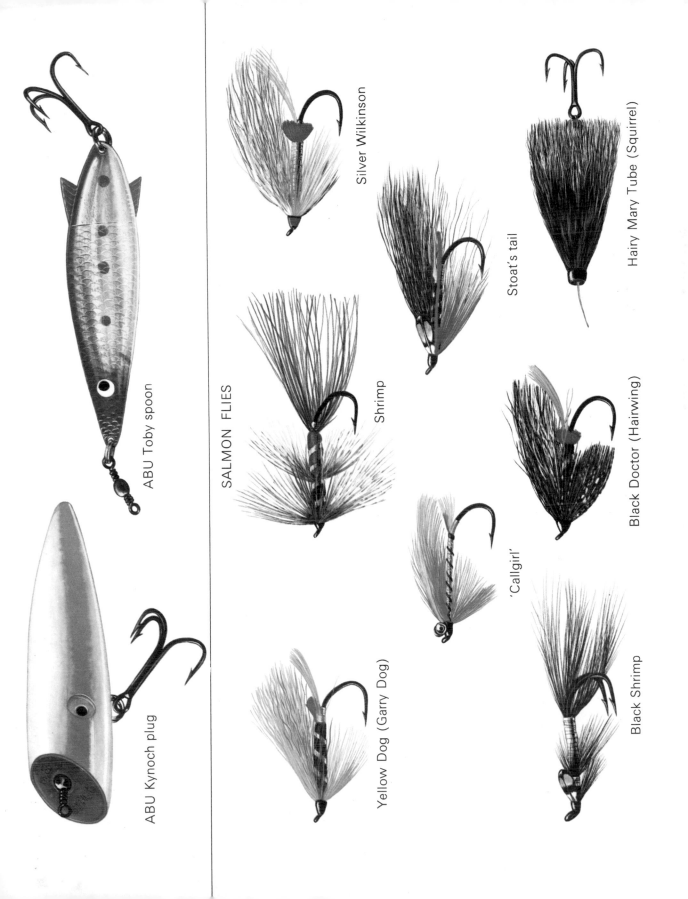

ABU Toby spoon

ABU Kynoch plug

SALMON FLIES

Silver Wilkinson

Hairy Mary Tube (Squirrel)

Stoat's tail

Shrimp

Black Doctor (Hairwing)

'Callgirl'

Yellow Dog (Garry Dog)

Black Shrimp

River Tay and Loch Tay, Kenmore. Salmon in lochs tend to travel well defined routes, generally close to the shoreline. Local knowledge of the main runs is even more important than in the river.

(a) Fish can be taken at the mouth of the river, where the loch begins to gain current.
(b) Other fish lie below the bridge and can be taken on spun baits.

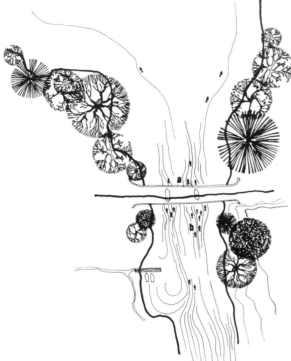

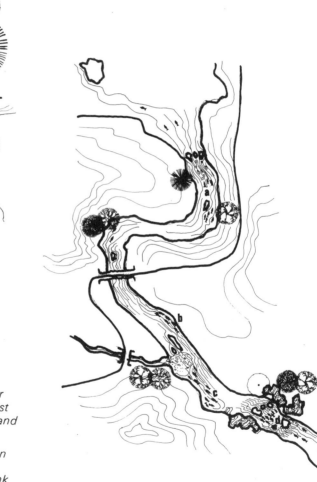

(Right).
Loch Ailsh and Upper River Oykel. This is summer and early autumn spate water, with small flies most successful. Summer grilse lie in shallow streams, and can be taken on fly from thinnest of water.

(a) Good taking lie where fish rest before final run into the loch.
(b) The 'Black Bank' — an overhanging peaty bank gives the salmon a protected lie. An excellent taking place with fish lying hard to the left bank.
(c) At the tail of the pool, the eddy on the right bank holds fish, which will sometimes take a fly facing 'downstream'.
(d) The pot between two falls is sufficiently large to fish with the fly, and often produces a taking fish.

pool (*d*). I had spent two weeks ghillying for a fine fisher from the south who every day had fished with skill and small flies to tempt fish from a river almost void of water. The fish were there but impossible to catch.

On the last day the sight of a couple of fishy tails showing in the dubb was too much. I tied on a weighted 3-inch yellow and orange tube fly — the sort of bait fit for the autumn Tay. Down it went and against all gentlemanly behaviour, rules of the river, and acceptable practice, I humbly admit to 'having a go'. I drew the fly quickly through the lie and as anticipated the fly stopped with a thump and a fish was on. I passed the rod to my guest.

The fish came out of the pool into the fast water, and off down the stream, just what one would expect from a foul-hooked fish. Eventually it tired and we beached a fine ten-pounder — the fly firmly embedded in the scissors!

One fish was enough, and even with the success of finding a ridiculously large gaudy fly accepted by a salmon we didn't repeat the experiment. Since that day I have on occasions during difficult low water fished properly with a fly much larger than conditions would indicate, frequently with success. Orange and yellow are successful colours, and I can't help thinking that the fly is taken as a representation of a prawn — hence the bigger bait still being attractive.

16. THE UPPER BEATS

As the salmon moves farther and farther upstream, so the river takes on a different character. Pools are smaller, streams are thinner, and there is generally less cover for the fish. Their character changes also. They have been in fresh water for some time, and will on their journey have come across a number of artificial baits which have been successfully avoided. They have gained experience; their cunning has increased. They will also be closer to spawning, and as such could well be more irritable, excitable, or just plain cautious. In any event, anything other than a stealthy approach to your fishing will meet with failure. Light tackle, and a concealed angler will bring rewards.

Any obstruction on the upper river, such as a difficult waterfall or rapids (page 31) will build up a large concentration of fish, especially in the colder water of spring, where fish will not move over the obstacle until the temperature increases (conversely the oxygen content decreases). One famous highland stream has little to obstruct spring running fish until the headwaters. Consequently, the fish run quickly through the lower river, straight through the loch and on to the upper tributary, all in a matter of hours. Vast falls prevent the fish from moving farther upstream, and the fishing in the falls pool and immediately downstream can be fantastic. Where else on a fly-only water can you see three rods in action at the one time playing fish? I had unfortunately been fishing two days before, when the river was bank high and, to any sensible salmon angler, totally unfishable. If you've done a round trip of six hundred miles, have only a couple of days on one of the finest stretches of salmon water in the world, it doesn't matter if you have to row across the fields to find the river, you still want to give it a try.

The same pool produced a fish for me the following spring. I had stepped out of my car six-and-a-half hours after leaving Edinburgh, walked up the bank, and was beckoned across to the far bank. I negotiated the falls on two footbridges and joined my Orkney friend. Teddy had just cast across the pool and handed me the rod. No, the four rods had not touched a fish all day. My hand just reached for the line as the fish pulled the belly tight, and the rod thumped down as the fish screamed across the pool. No, he wouldn't take the rod back, I'd have to play the bloody salmon myself. I was still driving, not fishing. The sea lice on the fish showed how long the salmon had taken to run the length of the river. What a catch! I wasn't even supposed to be on the water until the following day; I presented the salmon to my generous host.

Typical section on a bend in a salmon river — a small highland stream in the upper reaches.
Fish will not be here until summer and early autumn, and show a preference for well oxygenated water at the head of streams. Salmon also lie well under the banks, giving protection from sun and bright light. Pools which appear untenanted will often have fish lying in the thin stream water with their backs barely covered, and others will be under the 'outside' bank where the bank erosion will have formed a protective hole for resting fish.

(a) In early morning and again at dusk, fish will move on to the slacker edge of the stream, and even drop down to the tail of the pool. Sea trout frequently do this to feed at these times, and salmon will follow.

A 'commando' type approach is the only chance the angler will have of moving a fish in these circumstances, and only then when the tackle is fine and the fly small.

The fish under the bank pose a more difficult problem, and have to be approached from the opposite bank. A sunk fly, size according to water strength and height is an obvious choice, although a small spoon or devon could also give success.

Where allowed, both prawn and worm can be deadly. On smaller waters, a little shrimp or bunch of worms will be less likely to disturb the pool.

A fish hooked on this type of stream will without exception move back right under the holding bank, and to get sufficient leverage on the salmon, the angler has to play the fish from the opposite bank.

Pool on the Upper Oykel (below).

(a) Main lie in stream behind boulder, with other fish running through, and rarely showing interest.
(b) Good taking point where current eases, fish lying on edge.
(c) Quieter water on far side of current will carry lying fish, but difficulty of presentation across stream.
(d) Again, bait has to be 'hung' over fast stream, and in fly fishing, the line is mended upstream to give the lure a chance of good presentation to the fish before being 'snatched' by the current.

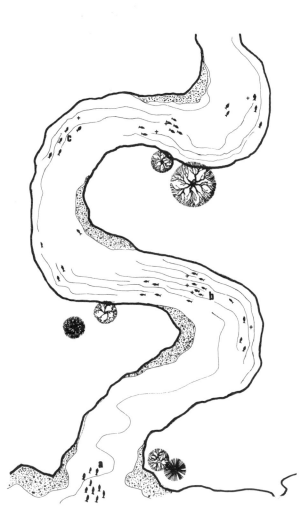

Classic falls pool on a highland river in Sutherland
(below).
This famous stretch of water produces fish from late
March on the fly in large numbers, fresh-run salmon
which run quickly through the lower river, through
the loch and into the upper reaches where this pool
lies. The spring fishing is particularly good, as the
falls discourage fish to run farther upstream until the
temperature warms up in late May.

(a) A deep pot, with fish lying hard to the left bank.
The fly has to be well sunk here, especially in the
early months.
(b) A shallower lie, but excellent taking place.
(c) Deceptive lie, with the narrow stream disguising
a deep hole close to the left bank where fish rest after
coming through the stream. They do, however, move
into the pool from the right bank, and can be picked
up there in the tail of the pool.
(d) Fish fan out across the stream here – an excellent
taking spot.
(e) Fish lie more to the right bank, and will take a fly
'backed up' the pool often better than a fly fished in
the traditional manner.
(f) Fish newly into the pool often show here, but
generally move quickly up into the main lies.
(g) Fish sometimes taken on the fly from stream
below bridge, but fish don't tarry long here.

Upper River Brora, a typical river/loch situation
(above).

(a) Small shoals of fish tend to move upstream
together, and even travel through lochs with the same
fish that they arrived with from the sea.
    If the angler is there at the right time, an otherwise
barren stretch with no real holding lies, can produce
excellent sport as the fish move through.
    It is possible to follow a group of fish for some
distance, and with luck take several salmon from the
same 'shoal'.
(b) Any quickening of the current through
constriction or obstruction will in a relatively slow
stretch of water produce taking lies. Not only do the
salmon hold in these places, but the angler's fly
'swims' better with the added flow.
(c) The outside of any bend will carry the deeper,
quicker water, and here generally, the angler's bait
will receive the most attention.

17. SALMON LAW

The Scottish Acts of 1424 and 1696 refer to the earliest legislation controlling the taking of salmon in Scotland. A series of Acts was passed between 1828 and 1868 which broadly provided for the setting up of District Fishery Boards, an annual close season of 186 days and a weekly close time of 36 hours, with reductions of the close time for fishing with rod and line. These Victorian Acts also provided that permission had to be granted by the proprietors of salmon fishing rights to persons wishing to take salmon, grilse, sea trout and whitling (small sea trout up to 1½ lb. in weight). They also recited the provisions of the earlier Scottish Act of 1696 prohibiting the slaughter of fry and smolts.

These acts were amended in 1951 by the Salmon Freshwater Fisheries (Protection) Scottish Act. Resulting from this legislation an angler wishing to fish for salmon and fish of the salmon kind must apply to the person with legal right for written permission.

The incidence of poaching, coupled with disease, in recent years has badly depleted spawning stock in the autumn months. Fortunately there is a hardening attitude to the poacher. The days of 'one for the pot' and the romanticism and excitement of the salmon poacher are gone. Today, there is big money for the organized gangs who steal our sport.

It was once suggested to me that if you were to take a moonlight walk by the banks of the Tweed any time after the fish build up towards spawning time, and blow a whistle, you'd be trampled in the stampede of bodies rushing away with their gaffs, weighted hooks and nets.

A 'Walkerburn Angel', as I discovered at a Tweedside hotel, is far from angelic. A wire trace loaded with a leaded hook is ripped across the backs of closely packed salmon.

I've even heard whisper of the morning bread van swopping its load of dough for a different kind in the shape of poached fish, collecting the night's catch from cottages and villages throughout the county. The total haul is then marketed through the 'back door', and hefty tax-free profits shared. And many of the hotels are to blame for accepting cut-price fish which they know to be taken illegally. Of course, they don't ask awkward questions. It's time the police did some questioning themselves!

18. SALMON ON A BUDGET

I was eighteen, had just left school, and could look forward to a long holiday before continuing my education at college. Most young anglers are financially limited far more than their mature counterparts, and to go salmon fishing, even at 10 shillings (50p) or £1 per day, at that stage meant careful budgeting and long waits between trips. To even think of those exclusive waters in the Highlands where a rod could cost anything up to 100 guineas a week was day dreaming — but dreaming about the impossible is a favourite pastime of mine, and I slowly developed a plan to get myself some first-class salmon fishing — legally — and even be paid for it to boot!

I had heard that a Sutherland estate employed both grouse beaters, and pony boys to help bring in the stags which were stalked and shot on the estate. The Oykel, a small but prolific salmon river known throughout Europe for the quality of its fishing, ran its entire length through

*The author fishing the famous Bridge Pool at Kelso
on the River Tweed in February 1973. In spite of
lowish water conditions, a big tube fly is necessary
to get down to the fish. On Tweed, the first fortnight
of February means fly only fishing, until the
commercial nets come on, on 15 February.*

the estate. The netting rights on the Dornoch
Firth at Bonar Bridge were also retained by the
estate, so that the correct balance was always
maintained: ample fish for the nets, fully but not
over-stocked pools for the guest angler. I wrote
to the factor and sporting manager, offering my
services as a salmon ghillie, and part-time pony
boy. I didn't really think I would get a job, and
nearly collapsed when I heard I was to walk such
famous pools, and be paid in addition a whole
£7.50!

Most of the guests were casual salmon fishers,
in some cases fishing, I'm sure, because they
regarded it as 'the thing to do'. Apart from
carrying tackle and ensuring the guest was as
comfortable as possible at all times, the ghillie
was there to point out the particular lies of the
salmon, where the guest might rise a fish, what
size of fly and pattern to select — all those pieces
of information which help the angler not
accustomed to a particular river to make his own
judgement about how he is going to tackle the
problems. It often went further, however, because
it soon became evident that a high percentage of
guests, if they could cast a fly, were not reacting
correctly to taking fish. Consequently, the pattern
for the day would often consist of an hour on the
first pool, where the guest would cast away, and
generally rise a fish with which he would not
connect, for one reason or another — perhaps
more than one fish would be hooked and lost, or
indeed no fish hooked or risen at all. In any case,
the procedure generally meant that the guest
then passed the rod to the ghillie to see if he
might fare better.

This was my fishing. Certainly, once a fish was
stalked, risen and hooked, the rod was offered
to the guest for him to play the fish; but few
would deny that the ultimate pleasure in salmon

fishing is the spectacular take and those first long seconds as the line draws, the rod is raised, and the return powerful signal is transmitted from an eruption of spray. Indeed, most guests were true sportsmen, since few would accept the offer of playing a fish, although it most certainly was their deserve since they were paying for the privilege. I remember one guest who had fished for ten days without so much as a rise — the problem had been lack of rain, and stale fish. He was a good angler, and I had had little opportunity to fish myself. On one of the occasions when I was fishing a thin stream, using the tiniest of Stoat's Tails, a heavy dirty-coloured fish had made a slow roll and taken the fly with it. On offering the rod to my guest I was told to land my own bloody fish, and if I needed assistance in the tailing of it, then he would be only too delighted to do so.

Few people have the time or the opportunity to act as ghillie on such an exclusive water but, on reflection, I now see all salmon fishing relatively. The chap who, for an outlay of £50, fishes a high-quality stretch of water stands a considerably better chance of getting a good number of fish, than the other angler who pays a pound for his day's fishing and catches nothing. Coupled with this is the problem of choosing the right time of the year. On a stretch of water which is not heavily fished, seasonal variation will not play such an important part as for those waters — such as angling association stretches — which may be tenanted by, collectively, a thousand or so anglers. What fish are lying in this water are very quickly acclimatized to the systematic angling approach, and consequently become uncatchable by legal means. It is probably through this kind of frustration on certain Border rivers that far too much sniggling (foul-hooking) is carried out, in spite of the attempts of commissioner and bailiff. It has reached such a peak on certain rivers that, in the autumn when pools become crowded with both fish and anglers, salmon become so restless that even new arrivals into the water will invariably remain aloof to the angler's fly, even when conditions would appear to be ideal.

As little as a year or two ago, there was salmon fishing available to the visitor to Scotland free of charge. Since the law states that written permission has first to be obtained, Perth Town Council issued day tickets, without charge, for the town water on the River Tay. This covered

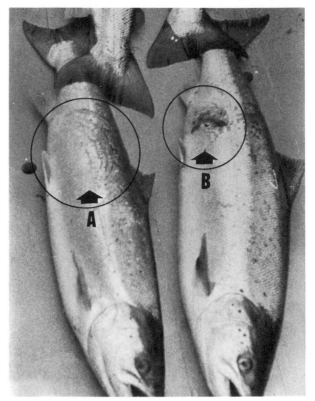

Two February 'springers' from the Kelso Junction Pool, attacked by estuary seals.

the letter of the law, and also ensured that numbers were restricted to a feasible level. The same ticket now costs around twenty-five pence, and in the early part of the year, and again in the autumn, fresh-run salmon are a real possibility, while herling (grilse sea trout) and brown and slob trout are around in good numbers. Like so much water which is near tidal, the long, flat, rather featureless pools are better spun than fished with the fly, but opportunity is there for both. Other stretches of this famous river are available from time to time to the visitor, but enquiries have to be made locally. During the summer months, the boats fishing many of the wider stretches of the river go off as sport slackens, and tickets on a part-seasonal basis are issued to the bank angler. It is at this time that the grilse and sea trout come into their own, and early morning or into dusk the angler can be well rewarded for his pound or two's outlay.

In terms of the angler from south of the border, those rivers most within his reach are the Tweed and tributaries on the east coasts, and the Solway rivers in the west — the main ones being the Nith and Annan. All these well-known rivers can offer the visiting angler salmon fishing for around a pound a day, or even less. A number of streams, given the correct season and sufficient rain, can yield superb catches of fish for a few pence.

One particular red-letter day which will remain with me the rest of my life was an embarrassingly absurd catch of eight sea trout, weighing 54 lb. They came from an overgrown stream which most anglers would normally pass by. The association controlling the water charged 2s. 6d. (12½p) a day to fish it. For ninety-five per cent of the season, parr and small trout were all that one would find, except, that is, for the occasional eel. Come the middle of September, and catch the river as it was dropping, EUREKA! Virtually impossible to fish with the fly; the best method was to trundle a lobworm under the overhanging trees. The water would be thinning chocolate, and as you worked your way slowly down under the trees, the steep bank high above your head, fish would be running the whole time. The worm would travel a yard, two yards, four or five — then stop! The twitching upstream movement would begin, and the angler would be into a sea trout — or sometimes a salmon, straight out of the sea. The association have now made the decision to close the stream at the end of

September and not the end of October as previously. It can be argued both ways: the fish can be left in peace to their spawning; over-ripe fish are not hooked; and the less sophisticated 'fisherman' is not tempted by over-stocked pools. However, one of the only two productive months so far as the angler is concerned is lost, fish will over-cut redds, and poachers will have free access to the river which would normally be tenanted.

The visitor to any river will have to work for his fish and if, indeed, he lands a single salmon, then he can be truly thankful. I fished the Tay on nine occasions last season, on a stretch which is restricted to three rods. Apart from kelts, caught right at the start of the season, the only activity I had was on my last visit when I took two cock fish. In working for his fish, the angler can do worse than to plan prior to being on the waterside, remembering two important things — seasonal variation, and the effect of rain, or lack of it, on the particular water selected. In many cases, the cheaper salmon water will at certain times of the year be about as full of salmon as your bath; turn on the tap, however, and later on you might just find the odd one!

Scotland for Fishing, the Scottish Tourist Board's publication, will tell you when to turn on the tap, and for how long . . . and where it is not going to cost you extra for the soap and towel.

19. HOW WAS YOUR SALMON YEAR

It started off reasonably enough, I suppose. On the Tay, where I had my first cast of the season, it was a miserable, wet, muggy sort of day, with low mist hugging the hills, not conducive to good sport in any way, but it was good to be out on the banks again.

We didn't really fish hard, and it wasn't surprising that none of us on that particular beat took a fish. Back at the hotel that evening, we had the pleasure of seeing two magnificent fresh-run fish taken from Kinnaird, a little downstream from us — the larger a splendid fish of well over 20 lb. What was missing in those early

days were the kelts that one used to curse as they hit the fly or spoon; always hoping for a springer, it was something of a disappointment to take a spent fish, but how I miss them now. I had twenty-two one day — 'a day of kelts', Bill Currie, who was fishing with me, once called it. Three of us had over fifty fish, and I managed the only springer of the day — my twenty-first fish — but the kelts gave us excitement and exhaustion.

I had eleven of them on the fly, coming at it from all directions, rolling over the fly, head and tailing beautifully, and in one case breaking the

line easily with a weighty flank. If you take a kelt in a day's fishing now, it is something of an occasion.

But the rivers stayed full and perhaps the Tay in particular ran big for as long as can be remembered right into the summer months when the river would normally have dropped well down. There was an absence of summer fish, small fish that is, the grilse, but they were more than made up for by the huge average weight of the salmon taken throughout the late spring and early summer. Bernard Blomefield had the best, from Scotland, a forty-four-pounder, but they had over twenty fish for their stay, weighing over 20 lb. apiece — a fantastic average, more akin to the returns shown in the books seventy years ago.

But then what happened? We went from too much water to no water at all and, consequently, salmon fishing for all but the lowest beats became a disaster. On many Scottish rivers this aggravated the disease situation, and the Nith in particular was hit badly early on with congested pools and little or no water to help spread the load. The rain came late, too late in many cases, such as the Tay, for the main beats to get much sport, but with it fish came, too. And in spite of disease and commercial netting, the fish still seemed to come, and many point to statistics and say: 'Where is the drop in fish catches? It's a myth.'

Perhaps we who don't see the kelts in the spring find it hard to understand, but for another season at any rate, salmon are still with us, and indeed many of my associates can point to one of their best seasons ever. My own first this season was to land four clean fish on the fly in one short afternoon spell — my best-ever fly catch on association water. The season for me on Tweed, as I write this, holds perhaps only one more short outing; providing the frosts hold and the river level drops to a more acceptable height, then I might still get that twenty-pounder on the fly which has eluded me for so long.

Twenty-four pounds of muscle — a firm cock fish from the Tweed in autumn, taken on a small shrimp tube.

20. THE INTERNATIONAL PICTURE

Canada

In the winter evenings, when the rod is hung up until the new season, the round of angling club socials begins. Often this means a film night. Trouble is, there are precious few films on angling available for club showing. I have written and produced a number in recent years, but we need many more.

Some of the best available come from Canada, and the game fishing for giant brook trout (they're really a kind of char) and Pacific and Atlantic salmon are spectacular.

A word of warning, though. As with expansion in the industrial areas of Europe, such as the Rhine, so pollution and abstraction are taking away more of the Canadian salmon fishing.

Off Newfoundland and the great rivers, they fish salt water for salmon, and many are caught on Scottish-produced flies which are trolled for these fish. Experimenting with salmon in the sea could give us a new sport round the British Isles, but the question of the legal right to fish would still appear to rest with the riparian owner of the lands surrounding the rivers to which the salmon three miles out to sea are heading.

Norway

I've several times tried to fish salmon in Norway. I now know that I'll have to be very rich or have the time and money to take a light aircraft north from Bergen to the lesser fished waters. There for ten pounds a day I can find good sport.

All the accessible rivers are very expensive, and largely unavailable to the casual visitor. There are exceptions, however, and the sizes of Norwegian salmon are enough to make the effort of fishing worthwhile.

I was invited to fish the Sand River whilst in Stavanger a year or two ago. What was the warmest summer for many years produced a situation which was, on the face of it, contradictory. No rain for weeks, but the rivers were unfishable — too high and continuously in spate.

Being snow-fed from the mountains, the warm weather had produced far more water than the angler wanted, and fishing was poor as a result.

Sweden

In Sweden, I met the opposite conditions on the Morrum which flows into the Baltic. More sea trout than salmon run this fine river, but since they average far heavier than many salmon, the techniques are the same.

The fishing on the beat I fished, near Abu Svangsta's famous factory, was a strange mixture of weeded streams and smooth, powerful glides. The fish were huge. Our best of the first evening weighed over eight kilos (that's around 17 lb.) — not a salmon, a hen sea trout, taken on a Swedish 'Toby', of course.

Iceland

Abu's film of *Salmon in Laxa* gives us a quick look at the superb salmon waters of Iceland.

I remember in 1968 having to choose between marrying Ruth, my wife, and going to Iceland. She should be eternally grateful, but still gets upset if I choose to slip over the hill for ten minutes after an evening trout — perhaps fishing every night is too much.

In 1974, the European Sea Angling Championships were held in Iceland — I made the trip this time.

Ireland

So much like Scotland!

It's rather like going home. Most years I manage a quick trip to County Mayo in June, basically a sea fishing trip. The Mayfly were off Lough Mask and the trout just about uncatchable. The sea trout and summer salmon were not quite up from the sea, and the early spring fish were a little stale. As I said, it was basically a sea-fishing trip.

I went back in early September. The sea-

Caught in the act! Migratory fish on our rivers not only run the gauntlet of estuary seals, commercial nets, otters, anglers and disease, but worst of all, that human disease, POACHING.

These two 'fishers' were spotted early one summer morning on a Scottish stream. Their identity is concealed because even photographic 'evidence' such as this would not convict. Moreover, the cameraman could well find himself on the receiving end of legal action — if not in the river!

fishing was great, the brown trout catchable, and a trout fly rod on the Newport River which flows into Clew Bay gave incredible sport.

The rain was lashing down as we stopped the car. A wee, tall fellow in a green hat full of 'fleas' came rushing across, rod in hand. He hadn't a coat, and water was forming a river down the back of his neck. I expected a fish to run upstream out of his shirt-back at any second.

'Quick mate, the fish are goin' mad,' he sang, '. . . dare out of dare tiny minds!' He rushed off, shouting behind him to be sure to add a black spider to the cast, one with silver tinsel and a red tag!

The water was slightly coloured and my false cast to lengthen line produced a firm take barely a rod-length from my feet. It was the first of sixteen sea trout to my 9-ft. cane rod before dusk. I lost the salmon which boiled at my black spider, and rushed off downstream back to the many islands of Clew Bay. There were many salmon there; it was the richness and eagerness of the sea trout which kept the 'fish' away from my flies. Some day I must return.

21. TAILPIECE - SALMON OR TROUT

I haven't been lucky enough to take a really big salmon, but perhaps a grilse the size of a trout is interesting enough.

What fascinates me is the overlap between salmon and sea trout and how one can fish for them. At either end of the scale, they are poles apart. But somewhere in the middle there is an affinity, a coming together of ideas which can benefit the angler after both species.

One October, Peebleshire Association Water was very low. My schoolboy knowledge accepted the advice of the local tackle dealer — there were no salmon but perhaps a sea trout. Just fish your trout rod and a tiny fly.

The wee ½-inch Stoat's Tail was taken by a salmon which stretched my resourceful 5 lb. cast and light-weight wand to their limits.

In November, the fish had arrived in numbers and I changed to my 13-foot fly rod and bigger tube. Bang, and a 9 lb. sea trout had me heading

seawards. At 9 lb. 2 oz. it turned out to be my best sea trout on the fly.

A small west coast burn — you can jump over it in places — receives a back end run of salmon and trout. It is overgrown and worm is the best if not the only bait to use. The salmon run quickly through from the loch below, and are not long in from the sea. The hen sea trout also arrive freshly from the sea. Cock sea trout, big fish, have the appearance of an earlier arrival in the loch before completing the spawning run to the upper river. They are magnificent fish, rich, red and spotted with powerful jaws and square tails. I took eight of them one day and a salmon. The 'fish' weighed 6 lb.; the sea trout totalled 54 lb., the best weighing 11½ lb., 10 lb., and 9¼ lb. My mind went back to that superb Charles Ritz photograph of two Em sea trout averaging about 20 lb. apiece. Where does salmon fishing stop and sea trout begin?